Literacy and Language
Progress Tests
3 & 4

Year 3 & 4 / Primary 4 & 5

Series developed by
Ruth Miskin

Written by
**Jenny Roberts,
Nick Cannon and
Susan Aykin**

Assessment Consultant
Susan Aykin

OXFORD
UNIVERSITY PRESS

Supporting you with the 2016 Assessments

OXFORD
UNIVERSITY PRESS

Great Clarendon Street, Oxford, OX2 6DP,
United Kingdom

Oxford University Press is a department of the University of Oxford. It furthers the University's objective of excellence in research, scholarship, and education by publishing worldwide. Oxford is a registered trade mark of Oxford University Press in the UK and in certain other countries

© Oxford University Press 2015

The moral rights of the authors have been asserted

First Edition published in 2015

British Library Cataloguing in Publication Data

Data available

ISBN: 978-0-19-836736-9

3 5 7 9 10 8 6 4 2

Paper used in the production of this book is a natural, recyclable product made from wood grown in sustainable forests. The manufacturing process conforms to the environmental regulations of the country of origin.

Printed and bound in Great Britain by Ashford Colour Press, Gosport, Hants

Oxford OWL

For teachers
Helping you with free eBooks, inspirational resources, advice and support

For parents
Helping your child's learning with free eBooks, essential tips and fun activities

www.oxfordowl.co.uk

Acknowledgements

Illustrations by Leo Broadley, Lesley Danson, Sheena Dempsey, Sarah Edmonds, Katie May Green, Freya Hartas, Simon Mendez, Matt Partridge, Sara Sanchez, Rachel Saunders and Briony May Smith

The publishers would like to thank the following for the permission to reproduce photographs:

p62: Arvind Balaraman/Shutterstock; Denis Kuvaev/Shutterstock; Marcos Mesa Sam Wordley/Shutterstock; Samuel Borges Photography/Shutterstock; p63: Leah-Anne Thompson/Shutterstock; Sonataphoto/Shutterstock; Triff/Shutterstock; p64: Kzenon/Shutterstock; Yodchompoo/Shutterstock; Dave King/Getty Images; p65: Justin Sullivan/Getty Images; Denis Radovanovic/Shutterstock; p74: Andrey Burmakin/Shutterstock; p75: TsuneoMP/Shutterstock; p76: Stephen Coburn/Shutterstock; thomas Koch/Shutterstock; p77: Pim Leijen/Shutterstock; Mondadori/Getty Images; p112: Pathompong Chai-onnom/Shutterstock; SurangaSL/Shutterstock; p113: Aditya Singh/Shutterstock; Signature Message/Shutterstock; p114: chrupka/Shutterstock; p115: Joe Amon/Getty Images; Monkey Business Images/Shutterstock

We are grateful for permission to include the following copyright material:

Floella Benjamin: extract from *Coming to England: An Autobiography* (Walker Books, 2009), copyright © Floella Benjamin 1995, reprinted by permission of Benjamin-Taylor Associates.

Alison Chisholm: 'About Knees', copyright © Alison Chisholm 2000, first published in *The Works* edited by Paul Cookson (Macmillan, 2000), reprinted by permission of the author.

Gillian Cross: extract from *The Demon Headmaster* (Oxford University Press, 2009), copyright © Gillian Cross 1982, reprinted by permission of Oxford University Press.

Heather Dyer: extract from *The Fish in Room 11* (Chicken House, 2013), text copyright © Heather Dyer 2004, 2005, reprinted by permission of Chicken House Ltd. All rights reserved.

Alexander McCall Smith: extract from *Akimbo and the Lions* (Egmont UK, 1992), copyright © Alexander McCall Smith 1992, reprinted by permission of Egmont UK Ltd, London and David Higham Associates.

Michael Morpurgo: extract from 'The Beastman of Ballyloch', first published in *Beyond the Rainbow Warrior* (Pavilion, 1997) and in *From Hearabout Hill* (Mammoth, 2000), copyright © Michael Morpurgo 1997, reprinted by permission of Egmont UK Ltd, London, and David Higham Associates.

Brian Patten: 'Dear Mum' from *Thawing Frozen Frogs* (Frances Lincoln, 2011), copyright © Brian Patten 1990, reprinted by permission of the author c/o Rogers, Coleridge & White Ltd, 20 Powis Mews, London W11 1JN.

Mal Peet and Elspeth Graham: extract from *Painting Out the Stars* (Walker Books, 2011), copyright © Mal Peet and Elspeth Graham 2011, reprinted by permission of Walker Books Ltd, London SE11 5HJ, www.walker.co.uk.

Jeremy Strong: extract from *Dinosaur Pox* (Puffin Books, 1999), copyright © Jeremy Strong 1999, reprinted by permission of David Higham Associates.

We have tried to trace and contact all copyright holders before publication. If notified, we will be pleased to rectify any errors or omissions at the earliest opportunity.

Contents

Introduction

What are the Read Write Inc. Literacy and Language Progress Tests?

The *Literacy and Language Progress Tests* are ideal for preparing children for the National Curriculum Tests in England. Drawing upon best-loved children's texts, they enable you to consolidate and assess grammar and punctuation, reading comprehension and writing from Years 2–6.

This Handbook contains all the resources you will need for Years 3 and 4 (Primary 4 and 5). The *Literacy and Language Progress Tests* comprise three handbooks plus online materials:

Handbook 2	Handbook 3 and 4	Handbook 5 and 6
This Handbook contains all the resources you will need for Year 2, and should be used alongside *Read Write Inc. Literacy and Language 2* resources.	This Handbook contains all the resources you will need for Years 3 and 4, and should be used alongside *Read Write Inc. Literacy and Language 3 and 4* resources.	This Handbook contains all the resources you will need for Years 5 and 6, and should be used alongside *Read Write Inc. Literacy and Language 5 and 6* resources.

Online resources

The additional resources available online include:

- Practice Assessment Papers for the end of Key Stage assessments that are closely matched to the content and format of the Key Stage 1 and Key Stage 2 National Curriculum Tests.
- Assessment Progress Trackers which show how these practice and assessment resources relate to the yearly expectations of the curriculum.

You can find them on www.oxfordowl.co.uk in the 'Teaching and Assessment' resources for *Read Write Inc.*

The key purpose of this resource is to allow you to assess knowledge taught with *Literacy and Language 3 and 4*, and to give children extra practice and consolidation where necessary. Ultimately, this is to ensure that children are confident independent readers and ambitious writers, and that they are fully prepared for the Reading Comprehension and English Grammar, Punctuation and Spelling assessments.

For the teaching and assessment of spelling, see the *Read Write Inc. Spelling* programme.

Overview of resources

Grammar and punctuation

Grammar Cards

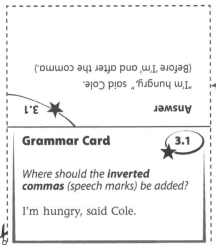

(Before 'I'm' and after the comma.)

"I'm hungry," said Cole.

Answer ⭐ 3.1

Grammar Card (3.1) ⭐

*Where should the **inverted commas** (speech marks) be added?*

I'm hungry, said Cole.

> Each Handbook contains a set of Grammar Cards to be used in the team Grammar Card Game. The game is a quick warm-up activity that allows you to assess which concepts the children need to practise more. For more detail, see p.9.

Grammar Assessments

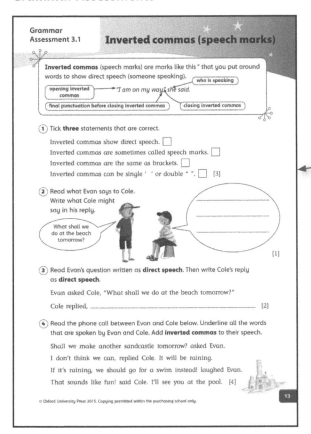

Grammar Assessment 3.1 — **Inverted commas (speech marks)**

Inverted commas (speech marks) are marks like this " " that you put around words to show direct speech (someone speaking).

opening inverted commas → *"I am on my way," she said.* ← who is speaking

final punctuation before closing inverted commas | closing inverted commas

(1) Tick **three** statements that are correct.

Inverted commas show direct speech. ☐
Inverted commas are sometimes called speech marks. ☐
Inverted commas are the same as brackets. ☐
Inverted commas can be single ' ' or double " ". ☐   [3]

(2) Read what Evan says to Cole. Write what Cole might say in his reply.

What shall we do at the beach tomorrow?

[1]

(3) Read Evan's question written as **direct speech**. Then write Cole's reply as **direct speech**.

Evan asked Cole, "What shall we do at the beach tomorrow?"

Cole replied, _____ [2]

(4) Read the phone call between Evan and Cole below. Underline all the words that are spoken by Evan and Cole. Add **inverted commas** to their speech.

Shall we make another sandcastle tomorrow? asked Evan.
I don't think we can, replied Cole. It will be raining.
If it's raining, we should go for a swim instead! laughed Evan.
That sounds like fun! said Cole. I'll see you at the pool.   [4]

© Oxford University Press 2015. Copying permitted within the purchasing school only.

13

> Each Handbook contains a set of photocopiable Grammar Assessments which provide focused practice and consolidation of the key grammar concepts for the year. For a list of the concepts included, see the chart on p.7.
>
> Ask children to complete these during your assessment week after you have taught the concept in *Literacy and Language,* if you feel they need more practice. The Grammar Card Game also acts as a diagnostic check to enable you to see which Grammar Assessments the children may need to complete.
>
> Mark Schemes are provided for all of the Grammar Assessments to save time when checking these. The marks for each question are shown in brackets and the marks for each Grammar Assessment add up to ten.

End of Year Grammar Test

The End of Year Grammar Test enables you to quickly check children's understanding of the key grammar concepts taught in Years 3 and 4 of *Literacy and Language* (which are also the key concepts listed in Years 3 and 4 of the Curriculum for England). This test can also be used to assess and place late starters to the school.

Reading comprehension

Reading Assessments

It was a dinosaur that got out of bed the next day – a dinosaur with fat, stumpy legs like thick tree trunks. Instead of freckles, she had purple and green blotches all over her fat, scaly body. She had a long thick tail. She had great leathery plates sticking out of her back, like fins that had been designed by somebody who couldn't draw. She had a small head with little red glinting eyes, a long snout and an even longer thick purple tongue.

Jodie knew something was wrong the moment she woke up. She struggled across to her mirror.

'Oh, isn't that just great,' she muttered. 'I'm a dinosaur. Just my luck. Why does nothing nice ever happen to me? First I'm given freckles and horrible hair, and now I've turned into a dinosaur.'

She suddenly had a thought. Maybe she *had* stared at herself in the mirror too long, just like Mark said.

69

There are six photocopiable Reading Assessments for each year:

- three fiction extracts from children's literature
- one poem
- two non-fiction texts.

The texts are by best-loved children's authors and poets and are linked by theme, genre or author to the texts in the units of *Literacy and Language*.

Each text is accompanied by a set of questions. The questions check children's comprehension of the texts and are written in the style of the questions that children will encounter in the Key Stage 2 National Curriculum Tests, to familiarise them with the form of these.

See p.8 for an overview of the Reading Assessments. For more detailed guidance, see p.54.

Writing composition

Writing Assessment Banks

The Writing Assessment Banks comprise:

- Suggested independent writing tasks for children, linked to their work in *Literacy and Language,* which allow you to assess children's writing in an unsupported context.
- Evaluation criteria to share with children before they complete these tasks, to help focus your marking.

For more detailed guidance on the Writing Assessment Banks, see p.137.

Assessment Progress Trackers with objectives from the curriculum requirements for writing are provided online. You can find them on <u>www.oxfordowl.co.uk</u> in the 'Teaching and Assessment' resources for *Read Write Inc.*

When should the Progress Tests be used?

We recommend that you have an assessment week every half term, and use the resources flexibly to suit your needs at that time, depending on which units you have taught so far.

The Year 3 and 4 overviews are given below.

In *Literacy and Language* grammar is taught in context, alongside the development of writing, comprehension and spoken language. These Progress Tests are for practice, consolidation and assessment of grammar, reading and writing **after** the main teaching in *Literacy and Language*. The assessments are linked by theme and subject to the texts and activities in *Literacy and Language*, to ensure that a context is maintained throughout the assessments.

Year 3

After *Literacy and Language* Unit...	Key grammar focus in *Literacy and Language*	Grammar Card Game	Grammar Assessments	Reading Assessments	Writing Assessment Bank
1	Adverbs and adverbials Inverted commas Headings and subheadings	Year 3 Units 1 and 2 cards	3.1 Inverted commas (speech marks)	Reading Assessment 3.1	Unit 1
2	Adverbs of time		3.2 Adverbs of time and place	Reading Assessment 3.2	Unit 2
3	Determiners *a* and *an* Conjunctions Adverbs and adverbials	Year 3 Units 3 and 4 cards	3.3 Determiners: *a* and *an* 3.4 Subordinating conjunctions	Reading Assessment 3.3	Unit 3
4	Prefixes		3.5 Prefixes	Reading Assessment 3.4	Unit 4
5	Adverbs and word families Sentences Perfect tense	Year 3 Units 5 and 6 cards	3.6 Word families 3.7 Verbs in perfect form	Reading Assessment 3.5	Unit 5
6	Prepositions Paragraphs		3.8 Prepositions 1 3.9 Prepositions 2 3.10 Clauses 3.11 Subordinate clauses	Reading Assessment 3.6	Unit 6
	At the end of the year: End of Year Grammar Test 3				

Year 4

After *Literacy and Language* Unit...	Key grammar focus in *Literacy and Language*	Grammar Card Game	Grammar Assessments	Reading Assessments	Writing Assessment Bank
1	Inverted commas	Year 4 Units 1 and 2 cards	4.1 Punctuating speech	Reading Assessment 4.1	Unit 1
2	Paragraphs		4.2 Paragraphs to organise ideas	Reading Assessment 4.2	Unit 2
3	Adverbials	Year 4 Units 3 and 4 cards	4.3 Adverbials and fronted adverbials	Reading Assessment 4.3	Unit 3
4	Prefixes		4.4 Apostrophes for possession	Reading Assessment 4.4	Unit 4
5	Standard English	Year 4 Units 5 and 6 cards	4.5 Standard English	Reading Assessment 4.5	Unit 5
6	Nouns and pronouns		4.6 Nouns and pronouns 4.7 Expanded noun phrases 4.8 Determiners 4.9 Possessive determiners 4.10 Possessive pronouns	Reading Assessment 4.6	Unit 6
	At the end of the year: End of Year Grammar Test 4				

Can I use the Progress Tests flexibly?

You can use the resources in a flexible order if you wish. Do ensure, however, that you have taught the relevant grammar concepts from *Literacy and Language* before giving children the Grammar Assessments (see chart on p.7).

You may wish to re-visit concepts from earlier years, if you feel children need to consolidate their understanding of these.

How do we ensure all children make progress? (differentiation)

The last question on each Grammar Assessment is often the most challenging. This is marked with a small shooting star to indicate that it is a stretch question.

The Reading Assessment Papers, as for the National Curriculum Tests, contain a mix of more straightforward and more challenging questions requiring inference, deduction and evidence. The marks for each question are shown in brackets. Again, particularly stretching questions are marked with a shooting star.

The Grammar Card Game encourages children to coach each other with grammar concepts, allowing the quicker-progress children to help those who need more help and consolidation with the grammar.

In addition, there is a bank of Challenge Activities online for children who need more stretch. You can find them on www.oxfordowl.co.uk in the 'Teaching and Assessment' resources for *Read Write Inc.*

Overview of Year 3 Reading Assessments

Unit	Text	Title and author
1	Fiction	*The Fish in Room 11* by Heather Dyer
2	Non-fiction (information text)	'Unusual Hobbies' by Adrian Bradbury
3	Fiction	*Dinosaur Pox* by Jeremy Strong
4	Non-fiction (explanation)	'How Do Submarines Work?' by Adrian Bradbury
5	Fiction – poetry	'About Knees' by Alison Chisholm
6	Fiction	*Akimbo and the Lions* by Alexander McCall Smith

Overview of Year 4 Reading Assessments

Unit	Text	Title and author
1	Fiction	*The Demon Headmaster* by Gillian Cross
2	Fiction – poetry	'Dear Mum' by Brian Patten
3	Fiction	'The Beastman of Ballyloch' by Michael Morpurgo
4	Non-fiction (persuasive text)	'Save the Elephants of Vietnam' by Liz Miles
5	Fiction	'Cloud Tea Monkeys' by Mal Peet and Elspeth Graham
6	Non-fiction (autobiography)	*Coming to England* by Floella Benjamin

Explanation of Grammar Card Game

Preparation

Decide which cards you would like children to use for the game. Choose up to ten cards each time. You may wish to include cards from the previous years where relevant, to ensure that children are continually re-visiting previous concepts.

Print the Grammar Card sheets on pp.10–12 or pp.33–35. You will need one set for each group of children (see below). Cut them up and fold them over to make cards (either sticking or laminating).

Grammar Card Game

Purpose: to assess which grammar concepts children are confident with and which may need re-teaching; to allow children to answer grammar questions in a group, coaching each other where appropriate

Organise children into groups – ideally four children per group (maximum six per group).

This game works in a similar way to Team Teach in *Read Write Inc. Spelling*. Nominate one child in the group to be the caller.

The caller will read out, or show, the question to the members of the group. (Whether the question is read out or shown will depend on the nature of the question. Children in the group can ask to see any question if this is helpful to them when considering the answer.) The children in the group respond by giving the answer. Alternatively, the children can discuss their thoughts together, and decide on an answer as a group.

The caller can check the answer as it is written on the back of the card. Ensure that the caller knows they must cover the back of the card when they read or show the question, so that they do not give away the answer. Children can check their own work.

If the children get a question right, it will go in one pile. Wrong answers will go in another pile. As you walk around the classroom and monitor children, use the game as a way to assess where a point may need to be re-taught or consolidated.

Group scores

You may wish to count up group scores and award rewards for these, to encourage children to help and coach each other.

After the game

By monitoring the children as they play the game – listening to their discussions and seeing which cards go in the 'incorrect' pile – you can assess which concepts the children need to consolidate further using the Grammar Assessments.

3.1

Grammar Card

Where should the **inverted commas** (speech marks) be added?

I'm hungry, said Cole.

3.2

Grammar Card

Where should the **inverted commas** (speech marks) be added?

Would you like an ice cream? asked Mum.

3.1 Answer

"I'm hungry," said Cole.

(Before 'I'm' and after the comma.)

3.2 Answer

"Would you like an ice cream?" asked Mum.

(Before 'Would' and after the question mark.)

3.3

Grammar Card

Which word is an **adverb**?

We are going on a picnic tomorrow.

3.4

Grammar Card

Which word is an **adverb**?

Have you been to the park before?

3.3 Answer

tomorrow

3.4 Answer

before

3.5

Grammar Card

Which word is an **adverb**?

We looked everywhere for the kitten.

3.6

Grammar Card

Which word is an **adverb**?

Can we play outside?

3.5 Answer

everywhere

3.6 Answer

outside

3.8

Grammar Card

Is the missing word **a** or **an**?

I can see ———— kite in the sky.

★ 3.8

Answer

a

3.7

Grammar Card

Is the missing word **a** or **an**?

Here is ———— orange.

★ 3.7

Answer

an

3.10

Grammar Card

Is the missing word **so** or **because**?

I am wearing a hat ———— it is cold.

★ 3.10

Answer

because

3.9

Grammar Card

Which word is a **conjunction**?

I like butter but I don't like jam.

★ 3.9

Answer

but

3.12

Grammar Card

Add a **prefix** to the word 'star' to mean someone very famous.

★ 3.12

Answer

superstar

3.11

Grammar Card

Is a **prefix** added to the start or end of a word?

★ 3.11

Answer

start

3.13

Grammar Card

Which words are in the same **word family**?

teach school teachers children

3.13

Answer

teach, teachers

3.14

Grammar Card

Is the correct word **has** or **have**?

Chan _____ been to the museum.

3.14

Answer

has

3.15

Grammar Card

Which word is a **preposition**?

Their father climbed up the ladder.

3.15

Answer

up

3.16

Grammar Card

Which word is a **preposition**?

The boys played games during the day.

3.16

Answer

during

3.17

Grammar Card

Which is the **main clause**?

I gave Gran a card that I had made.

3.17

Answer

I gave Gran a card

3.18

Grammar Card

Which is the **subordinate clause**?

You can come too if you are ready.

3.18

Answer

if you are ready

Inverted commas (speech marks)

> **Inverted commas** (speech marks) are marks like this " that you put around words to show direct speech (someone speaking).
>
> opening inverted commas → "I am on my way," she said. ← who is speaking
>
> final punctuation before closing inverted commas
>
> closing inverted commas

1 Tick **three** statements that are correct.

Inverted commas show direct speech. ☐

Inverted commas are sometimes called speech marks. ☐

Inverted commas are the same as brackets. ☐

Inverted commas can be single ' ' or double " ". ☐   [3]

2 Read what Evan says to Cole. Write what Cole might say in his reply.

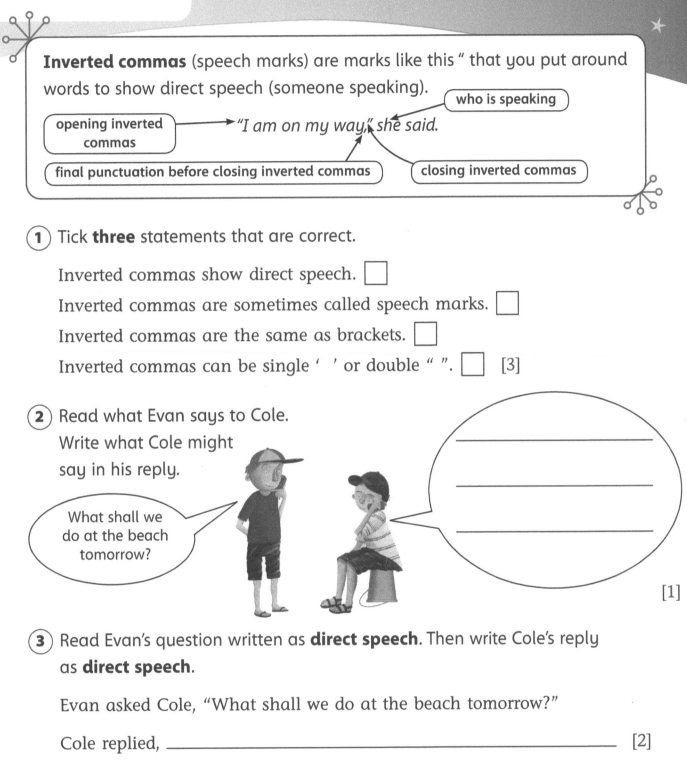

What shall we do at the beach tomorrow?

[1]

3 Read Evan's question written as **direct speech**. Then write Cole's reply as **direct speech**.

Evan asked Cole, "What shall we do at the beach tomorrow?"

Cole replied, _____   [2]

4 Read the phone call between Evan and Cole below. Underline all the words that are spoken by Evan and Cole. Add **inverted commas** to their speech.

Shall we make another sandcastle tomorrow? asked Evan.

I don't think we can, replied Cole. It will be raining.

If it's raining, we should go for a swim instead! laughed Evan.

That sounds like fun! said Cole. I'll see you at the pool.   [4]

Adverbs of time and place

> **Adverbs** can tell us *when* something happens or has happened.
> We call these 'adverbs of time', e.g. *after, finally, next, first, tomorrow.*

(1) Circle **four adverbs of time** in the text below.

Yesterday Lucy, Amy and Sam went
on a picnic. First they made some
sandwiches. Then they packed some
apples, cake and juice. Before they left,
Lucy grabbed an umbrella.   [4]

> **Adverbs** can also tell us *where* something happens or has happened. We call
> these 'adverbs of place', e.g. *upstairs, nearby, outside, everywhere.*

(2) Circle **four adverbs of place** in the text below.

Fib followed Lucy everywhere. When Lucy walked downstairs, Fib followed
her. When Lucy ran outside, Fib followed her. Even when Lucy played in the
park, Fib stood nearby.   [4]

(3) Complete the sentence below by choosing **two adverbs** from the box.

> inside   tomorrow   outside   yesterday

_____, Lucy played

_____ with Sam and Amy

in the park.   [2]

14

Determiners: *a* and *an*

We use the **determiner** *a* before a word that starts with a *consonant*.
We use *an* before a word that starts with a *vowel*.

(a consonant) *a robot*   *an invention* (a vowel)

Remember!

The vowels are *a, e, i, o, u*. Some people remember them with the phrase:
*an **a**ngry **e**lephant **i**n **o**range **u**nderpants.*

(1) Circle the correct **determiner** in bold in each sentence.
Think carefully about which is correct.

a. There was **a/an** fiery glint in her eyes.

b. Your room is **a/an** tip!

c. **A/An** orange spark flew off the robot's hand.

d. Robert's metallic features were creased into
a/an expression of sadness.

e. Standing by the sink was **a/an** girl robot.

f. Under Shannon's bed, Nita found **a/an** old,
half-eaten, mouldy sandwich.   [6]

(2) Complete the list by choosing
the correct words from the box.

(sock   umbrella   apple   bottle)

What we found under the bed:

an _____

a _____

an _____

a _____   [4]

Subordinating conjunctions

> **Subordinating conjunctions** link together a main clause and a subordinate clause. Some subordinating conjunctions show time or cause, e.g. *before, after, so, because.*

1 Circle the correct **conjunction** in bold in each sentence.

   a. Callum's room was a mess **so/because** his mum told him to tidy it.

   b. Mum told Callum to clean his teeth **before/after** he went to bed.   [2]

2 Circle the **subordinating conjunction** in each sentence.

   a. Callum shook Robert's hand carefully because it
   was made from barbecue skewers.

   b. Callum was dashing to school when he almost bumped into Robert.

   c. Robert looked sad after the children said he was weird.

   d. Shannon invited Callum to her house so he could meet Nita.   [4]

3 Complete each sentence by choosing the correct **subordinating conjunction**.

   after   while   before

   a. You must put on your socks _____ you put on your shoes.

   b. In the afternoon, _____ they have been to school, Robert and
   Callum visit Shannon and Nita.

   c. Callum drinks a milkshake _____ Robert cleans his bedroom.

                                                                          [3]

4 Write a sentence that includes the **subordinating conjunction** *because.*

   _____

   _____ [1]

Prefixes

A **prefix** is a group of letters that is added to the front of a word to change its meaning, e.g. *super-, anti-, auto-, micro-, pre-*.

1 Match up the **prefixes** and nouns to make new nouns.
The first one has been done for you.

Prefix	Noun
pre-	pilot
super-	school
auto-	glue
anti-	chip
micro-	clockwise [4]

2 Complete each sentence by choosing the correct **prefix**.

super-   pre-   micro-

a. The prefix _____ means big or great.

b. The prefix _____ means very small.

c. The prefix _____ means before.   [3]

3 Add a word to the prefixes below to create a new word.

a. super_____

b. micro_____

c. auto_____   [3]

Word families

Words that have the same root belong in the same family, e.g. *teach* and *teacher*. We call them **word families**.

1 Match the words that belong in the same **word family**.

jewels   complaint

angry   suspects

suspicion   jewellery

complaining   angrily   [4]

2 Circle **three words** in each list that belong in the same **word family**.

a. friends   trainers   fire   training   retrain   higher

b. lock   look   unlock   key   keen   locking

c. shriek   broken   break   smash   unbroken   lunch   [3]

3 Complete each sentence by choosing the correct word.

lemony   lemon   lemonade

a. An idea fizzed like shaken

_____ inside Adil's brain.

b. There is only one _____

left on our tree.

c. This cake tastes _____.   [3]

Verbs in perfect form

> We use the **perfect form** of a verb to talk about something that happened or started happening earlier. We use *has, have* or *had* with the main verb:
>
> Adil had noticed the beehive near the gates when they first arrived at Saxton Manor Museum.
>
> (verb in perfect form)

1 Circle the correct **verb form** in bold in each sentence below.

   a. Katie and Adil **has/have/had** spent all their holidays together, and still do now.

   b. Although Adil **has/have/had** noticed the beehive, he did not know what it was.

   c. Katie **has/have/had** wondered where Mrs McCreevy was, until she heard someone hammering on a door.

   d. The thief **has/have/had** been found out so now she is in prison.   [4]

2 Complete each sentence with *has, have* or *had*.

   a. Katie and Adil _____ given a statement so now they can go home.

   b. Adil _____ written down what happened so he can tell people at school about his adventure.

   c. The thief _____ not realised the bee sting would give her away.

   d. The other suspects _____ told Sergeant Pemberton that they think the children are very clever.   [4]

3 Think of some ideas to complete each sentence below.

   a. My brother and I have always _____ .

   b. Although Mum had _____ some pizza, she was still hungry.   [2]

Prespositions 1

> **Prepositions** are placed before nouns, noun phrases or pronouns. They can help to describe *where* things are or the *direction* they are going in.
>
> *He built the tree house high in the branches of an acacia tree.*
>
> preposition of place

(1) Circle **five prepositions** in the text below.

One day, the evil enchantress came and sat in the deep shade of the acacia tree. She knew that, above her head, three pairs of eyes gazed down at her.

"Little boys," she croaked, "let me come up the ladder and look inside your wonderful tree house." [5]

(2) Complete each sentence by choosing the correct **preposition**.

> at   up   under   into

a. He ran, howling, _____ the desert.

b. The enchantress climbed _____ the ladder, towards the tree house.

c. The father ran to the house of the wise man and threw himself _____ his feet.

d. He hid the golden drum _____ a cloak. [4]

(3) Complete the sentence by adding a **preposition**.

He could see three pairs of frightened eyes glowing _____ a dark corner. [1]

Prepositions 2

> **Prepositions** are placed before nouns, noun phrases or pronouns.
> They can show *time* or *relationship*.
>
> *The enchantress returned after the herdsman had left for work.*
>
> (preposition of time) (preposition of relationship)
>
> *The enchantress was punished for her wickedness.*

1 Tick **two** statements that are correct.

Prepositions show that someone is speaking. ☐

Prepositions are placed before nouns. ☐

Prepositions can show time or relationship. ☐ [2]

2 Circle **one preposition of time** in each sentence.

a. Before work, the herdsman warned his sons to stay safe.

b. The boys stayed in the tree until their father came home.

c. During the day, the boys would scamper about, as happy as can be.

d. The father had taken care of his sons since their mother died. [4]

3 Complete each sentence using 'because of', 'for' or 'from'.

a. The herdsman rubbed ash in his hair _____ his disguise.

b. He knew what to do _____ the wise man's words.

c. The boys' legs were still aching _____ the walk. [3]

4 Write down the **preposition** which would fit into both the phrases below.

_____

A bottle ▊▊▊▊ milk.

I have two pairs ▊▊▊▊ trainers. [1]

Clauses

A **clause** is a group of words which includes a verb. A clause can be a complete sentence or part of a sentence. This sentence has one clause:
The Earth is crowded.

This sentence has two clauses, joined by a conjunction:

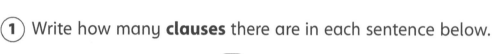

The Earth is crowded and the climate is changing.

first clause   conjunction   second clause

1 Write how many **clauses** there are in each sentence below.

a. We need more fuel. ☐

b. The population is growing. ☐

c. A meteor hit Earth and it killed off most living creatures. ☐

d. We need to explore other planets because our planet is too crowded. ☐

e. All living things need water. ☐   [5]

2 Circle the **conjunction** that joins the **clauses** in each sentence.

a. Some planets are too hot for us because they are close to the Sun.

b. Astronauts will travel to Mars but it will be a long journey.

c. Unmanned spaceships have landed on Mars and explored the planet.   [3]

3 Add another **clause** to finish each sentence.

a. I would like to go to Mars but _____ .

_____

b. People are looking for a new planet to live on because _____

_____ .   [2]

Subordinate clauses

A **clause** is a group of words which includes a verb. A **subordinate clause** helps to give more meaning to a main clause. It does not make sense on its own and it starts with a **subordinating conjunction**, e.g. *if, when, because, before.*

*Ben went to the space museum **because** he wanted to see the rockets.*

(main clause)   (subordinate clause, starting with subordinating conjunction)

(1) Circle the **subordinating conjunction** in each sentence.

a. The astronauts waved before they went into the spaceship.

b. When it is a clear night I like looking at the stars.   [2]

(2) Match each main clause with a **subordinate clause** to make a sentence.

Main clause	Subordinate clause
People will need another planet	because we need it to survive.
I want to be an astronaut	if Earth becomes too crowded.
The scientist did an experiment	that proved we need oxygen to live.
Water is important	when I grow up. [4]

(3) Underline the **subordinate clause** in each sentence.

a. If you want, we could go to the space museum.

b. She was in the army before she became an astronaut.

c. There is more water in the sea since the icebergs melted.

d. When you know where to look,
   you can see Mars in the night sky.   [4]

Grammar Assessment 3.1 **Inverted commas (speech marks)**

(1) **Award 1 mark** for each correct box ticked.

Inverted commas show direct speech. ☑

Inverted commas are sometimes called speech marks. ☑

Inverted commas are the same as brackets. ☐

Inverted commas can be single ' ' or double " ". ☑   **[3]**

(2) **Award 1 mark** for speech in the speech bubble without inverted commas, e.g.

Let's collect shells and swim in the sea.   **[1]**

(3) **Award 1 mark** for a pair of inverted commas (single or double) and **1 mark** for final punctuation within the inverted commas, e.g.

Cole replied, "Let's collect shells and swim in the sea."   **[2]**

(4) **Award 1 mark** for correct insertion of inverted commas (single or double) in each line of speech.

"Shall we make another sandcastle tomorrow?" asked Evan.

"I don't think we can," replied Cole. "It will be raining."

"If it's raining, we should go for a swim instead!" laughed Evan.

"That sounds like fun!" said Cole. "I'll see you at the pool."   **[4]**

Grammar Assessment 3.2 **Adverbs of time and place**

(1) **Award 1 mark** for each adverb of time identified.

(Yesterday) Lucy, Amy and Sam went on a picnic. (First) they made some sandwiches. (Then) they packed some apples, cake and juice. (Before) they left, Lucy grabbed an umbrella.   **[4]**

(2) **Award 1 mark** for each adverb of place identified.

Fib followed Lucy (everywhere.) When Lucy walked (downstairs,) Fib followed her. When Lucy ran (outside,) Fib followed her. Even when Lucy played in the park, Fib stood (nearby.)   **[4]**

(3) **Award 1 mark** for each correct adverb.

Yesterday, Lucy played **outside** with Sam and Amy in the park.   **[2]**

Grammar Assessment 3.3 Determiners: *a* and *an*

(**1**) **Award 1 mark** for each correct determiner.

a. There was (**a**)/**an** fiery glint in her eyes.

b. Your room is (**a**)/**an** tip!

c. **A**/(**An**) orange spark flew off the robot's hand.

d. Robert's metallic features were creased into **a**/(**an**) expression of sadness.

e. Standing by the sink was (**a**)/**an** girl robot.

f. Under Shannon's bed, Nita found **a**/(**an**) old, half-eaten, mouldy sandwich. **[6]**

(**2**) **Award 1 mark** for each item inserted next to the correct determiner.

an **umbrella**

a **sock**

an **apple**

a **bottle** **[4]**

Grammar Assessment 3.4 Subordinating conjunctions

(**1**) **Award 1 mark** for each correct conjunction.

a. Callum's room was a mess (**so**)/**because** his mum told him to tidy it.

b. Mum told Callum to clean his teeth (**before**)/**after** he went to bed. **[2]**

(**2**) **Award 1 mark** for each subordinating conjunction identified.

a. Callum shook Robert's hand carefully (**because**) it was made from barbecue skewers.

b. Callum was dashing to school (**when**) he almost bumped into Robert.

c. Robert looked sad (**after**) the children said he was weird.

d. Shannon invited Callum to her house (**so**) he could meet Nita. **[4]**

(**3**) **Award 1 mark** for each correct subordinating conjunction.

a. You must put on your socks **before** you put on your shoes.

b. In the afternoon, **after** they have been to school, Robert and Callum visit Shannon and Nita.

c. Callum drinks a milkshake **while** Robert cleans his bedroom. **[3]**

(**4**) **Award 1 mark** for the correct use of 'because' to link a main clause and a subordinate clause, e.g.

I am tired **because** I went to bed late last night. **[1]**

Grammar Assessment 3.5 **Prefixes**

(1) **Award 1 mark** for each prefix correctly matched to a noun.

Prefix	Noun
pre-	pilot
super-	school
auto-	glue
anti-	chip
micro-	clockwise

pre- → school
super- → glue
auto- → pilot
anti- → clockwise
micro- → chip **[4]**

(2) **Award 1 mark** for each correct answer.

a. The prefix **super-** means big or great.

b. The prefix **micro-** means very small.

c. The prefix **pre-** means before.   **[3]**

(3) **Award 1 mark** for each new word, e.g.

a. super**hero**

b. micro**wave**

c. auto**biography**   **[3]**

Grammar Assessment 3.6 **Word families**

(1) **Award 1 mark** for each pair of correctly matched words.

jewels	complaint
angry	suspects
suspicion	jewellery
complaining	angrily

jewels → jewellery
angry → angrily
suspicion → suspects
complaining → complaint   **[4]**

(2) **Award 1 mark** for each word family identified.

a. friends (trainers) fire (training) (retrain) higher

b. (lock) look (unlock) key keen (locking)

c. shriek (broken) (break) smash (unbroken) lunch   **[3]**

(3) **Award 1 mark** for each correct word.

a. An idea fizzed like shaken **lemonade** inside Adil's brain.

b. There is only one **lemon** left on our tree.

c. This cake tastes **lemony**.   **[3]**

Grammar Assessment 3.7 **Verbs in perfect form**

(1) **Award 1 mark** for each correct verb form.

a. Katie and Adil **has**/ (**have**) /**had** spent all their holidays together, and still do now.

b. Although Adil **has/have**/ (**had**) noticed the beehive, he did not know what it was.

c. Katie **has/have**/ (**had**) wondered where Mrs McCreevy was, until she heard someone hammering on a door.

d. The thief (**has**) /**have/had** been found out so now she is in prison. **[4]**

(2) **Award 1 mark** for each correct word.

a. Katie and Adil **have** given a statement so now they can go home.

b. Adil **has** written down what happened so he can tell people at school about his adventure.

c. The thief **had** not realised the bee sting would give her away.

d. The other suspects **have** told Sergeant Pemberton that they think the children are very clever. **[4]**

(3) **Award 1 mark** for each correct sentence, e.g.

a. My brother and I have always **enjoyed playing tennis**.

b. Although Mum had **eaten** some pizza, she was still hungry. **[2]**

Grammar Assessment 3.8 **Prepositions 1**

(1) **Award 1 mark** for each preposition identified.

One day, the evil enchantress came and sat (**in**) the deep shade of the acacia tree. She knew that, (**above**) her head, three pairs of eyes gazed (**down**) at her.

"Little boys," she croaked, "let me come (**up**) the ladder and look (**inside**) your wonderful tree house." **[5]**

(2) **Award 1 mark** for each preposition inserted correctly.

a. He ran, howling, **into** the desert.

b. The enchantress climbed **up** the ladder, towards the tree house.

c. The father ran to the house of the wise man and threw himself **at** his feet.

d. He hid the golden drum **under** a cloak. **[4]**

(3) **Award 1 mark** for any plausible preposition, e.g.

He could see three pairs of frightened eyes glowing **in** a dark corner. **[1]**

Grammar Assessment 3.9 **Prepositions 2**

(1) **Award 1 mark** for each correct box ticked.

Prepositions show that someone is speaking. ☐

Prepositions are placed before nouns. ☑

Prepositions can show time or relationship. ☑ **[2]**

(2) **Award 1 mark** for each preposition of time identified.

a. (Before) work, the herdsman warned his sons to stay safe.

b. The boys stayed in the tree (until) their father came home.

c. (During) the day, the boys would scamper about, as happy as can be.

d. The father had taken care of his sons (since) their mother died. **[4]**

(3) **Award 1 mark** for each correct preposition.

a. The herdsman rubbed ash in his hair **for** his disguise.

b. He knew what to do **because of** the wise man's words.

c. The boys' legs were still aching **from** the walk. **[3]**

(4) **Award 1 mark** for the correct preposition.

of **[1]**

Grammar Assessment 3.10 **Clauses**

(1) **Award 1 mark** for each correct answer.

a. We need more fuel. ☐1☐

b. The population is growing. ☐1☐

c. A meteor hit Earth and it killed off most living creatures. ☐2☐

d. We need to explore other planets because our planet is too crowded. ☐2☐

e. All living things need water. ☐1☐ **[5]**

(2) **Award 1 mark** for each conjunction identified.

a. Some planets are too hot for us (because) they are close to the Sun.

b. Astronauts will travel to Mars (but) it will be a long journey.

c. Unmanned spaceships have landed on Mars (and) explored the planet. **[3]**

(3) **Award 1 mark** for each new clause, e.g.

a. I would like to go to Mars but **I am scared of flying**.

b. People are looking for a new planet to live on because **our planet is overcrowded**. **[2]**

Grammar Assessment 3.11 **Subordinate clauses**

(1) Award 1 mark for each subordinating conjunction identified.

a. The astronauts waved (before) they went into the spaceship.

b. (When) it is a clear night I like looking at the stars.   **[2]**

(2) Award 1 mark for each main clause correctly matched to a subordinate clause.

Main clause	Subordinate clause
People will need another planet	because we need it to survive.
I want to be an astronaut	if Earth becomes too crowded.
The scientist did an experiment	that proved we need oxygen to live.
Water is important	when I grow up. **[4]**

(3) Award 1 mark for each subordinate clause identified.

a. <u>If you want</u>, we could go to the space museum.

b. She was in the army <u>before she became an astronaut</u>.

c. There is more water in the sea <u>since the icebergs melted</u>.

d. <u>When you know where to look</u>, you can see Mars in the night sky.   **[4]**

End of Year Grammar Test 3

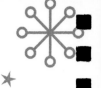

(1) Add the missing **inverted commas** (speech marks) to the sentence.

Can I help you to build that sandcastle? asked Evan.   [2]

(2) Circle **two adverbs** in the sentence below.

Yesterday, I sneezed loudly in the spelling test.   [2]

(3) Tick the correct word to complete the sentence.

You will need ⬚ umbrella because it is going to rain.

a ☐   an ☐   [1]

(4) Complete the sentence using **two conjunctions** from the box.

> but   and   or

You can ask Dylan _____ Ava to your party, _____ not both of them.

[2]

(5) Circle the **adverb** in the sentence below.

We looked everywhere for Nadir's rabbit.   [1]

(6) Circle the **two prepositions** in the sentence below.

I found him in a box, under some newspaper.   [2]

(7) Tick the correct word to complete the sentence.

Although the girl ⬚ said sorry, I am still sad.

have ☐

has ☐

is ☐   [1]

(8) Circle **three words** in the same **word family**.

working   walking   rework   worker   king   [3]

(9) Underline the **subordinate clause** in the sentence below.

James was quiet because he was sad.   [1]

(10) Match up the **prefixes** with the words. Then write the new words. The first one has been done for you.

auto-   star   _____

super-   pilot   <u>autopilot</u>

anti-   fix   _____

pre-   clockwise   _____   [3]

(11) Tick the correct **conjunction** to complete the sentence.

Charith chose a book ▮▮▮▮▮▮ he was in the bookshop.

so ☐

which ☐

when ☐

why ☐   [1]

(12) Circle the **preposition** in the sentence below.

Dad fell asleep during the play.   [1]

TOTAL MARKS: _____ / 20

1 **Award 1 mark** for each correct inverted comma (single or double).

"Can I help you to build that sandcastle?" asked Evan. **[2]**

2 **Award 1 mark** for each adverb identified.

(Yesterday) I sneezed (loudly) in the spelling test. **[2]**

3 **Award 1 mark** for the correct box ticked.

a ☐   an ☑ **[1]**

4 **Award 1 mark** for each conjunction correctly inserted into the sentence.

You can ask Dylan **or** Ava to your party, **but** not both of them. **[2]**

5 **Award 1 mark** for identifying the adverb.

We looked (everywhere) for Nadir's rabbit. **[1]**

6 **Award 1 mark** for each preposition identified.

I found him (in) a box, (under) some newspaper. **[2]**

7 **Award 1 mark** for the correct box ticked.

have ☐   has ☑   is ☐ **[1]**

8 **Award 1 mark** for each correct word identified.

(working)   walking   (rework)   (worker)   king **[3]**

9 **Award 1 mark** for correctly identifying the subordinate clause.

James was quiet <u>because he was sad</u>. **[1]**

10 **Award 1 mark** for each correct new word.

auto- ────── star   **superstar**

super- ────── pilot   autopilot

anti- ────── fix   **prefix**

pre-   ────── clockwise   **anticlockwise** **[3]**

11 **Award 1 mark** for the correct box ticked.

so ☐   which ☐   when ☑   why ☐ **[1]**

12 **Award 1 mark** for identifying the preposition.

Dad fell asleep (during) the play. **[1]**

Grammar Card 4.1

What missing **punctuation** should be added?

Are you tired asked the teacher.

4.1

Answer

"Are you tired?" asked the teacher.

(inverted commas [speech marks] and a question mark)

Grammar Card 4.2

What missing **punctuation** should be added?

I don't have it she said.

4.2

Answer

"I don't have it," she said.

(inverted commas [speech marks] and a comma)

Grammar Card 4.3

Is the missing word **pages** or **sentences**?

A paragraph is a group of ___.

4.3

Answer

sentences

Grammar Card 4.4

Which word is a **determiner**?

May I have that blue balloon?

4.4

Answer

that

Grammar Card 4.5

Which word is a **determiner**?

She had some lovely presents.

4.5

Answer

some

Grammar Card 4.6

Which word is a **determiner**?

Have you seen my cat?

4.6

Answer

my

4.8

Grammar Card

Change this sentence so it has a *fronted adverbial*.

They knocked on the door for five minutes.

4.8

Answer

For five minutes, they knocked on the door.

4.7

Grammar Card

Which phrase is an *adverbial*?

The Trolls partied all through the night.

4.7

Answer

all through the night

4.10

Grammar Card

Where should you add *punctuation* in this sentence?

The thiefs glove was found on the floor.

4.10

Answer

The thief's glove was found on the floor.

(an apostrophe to show that the glove belonged to the thief)

4.9

Grammar Card

Change this sentence so it has a *fronted adverbial*.

We sang a song before we left.

4.9

Answer

Before we left, we sang a song.

4.12

Grammar Card

Which words are an *expanded noun phrase*?

I saw the young Troll with huge green eyes.

4.12

Answer

the young Troll with huge green eyes

4.11

Grammar Card

Where should you add *punctuation* in this sentence?

The police officers uniforms were blue.

4.11

Answer

The police officers' uniforms were blue.

(an apostrophe to show that the uniforms belonged to the police officers)

4.14

Grammar Card

Is the missing word did or done?

I _____ something very brave today.

Answer

did

4.13

Grammar Card

Is the missing word was or were?

We _____ just looking for old coins.

Answer

were

4.16

Grammar Card

Which word is a pronoun?

Hamid waved goodbye as he got on the bus.

Answer

he

4.15

Grammar Card

Is the missing word them or it?

I saw the green bike and wanted _____ .

Answer

it

4.18

Grammar Card

Is the missing word he's or his?

I think that book is _____ .

Answer

his

4.17

Grammar Card

Is the missing word there's or theirs?

These coats are _____ .

Answer

theirs

Punctuating speech

Direct speech is the exact words being spoken by someone. We show this by using **inverted commas**.

opening inverted commas
closing inverted commas

"Your tea is ready," Mum called.

final punctuation within the inverted commas

We change the punctuation if we write who is speaking first, e.g. *Mum called, "Your tea is ready."*

(1) Add the correct punctuation to the sentences below.

a. I've got an idea Chandra said thoughtfully.

b. Taj, I've got something to show you Ravi said.

c. Ravi whispered to Chandra What's Mum talking about? Taj gets everything he wants

d. Our dad's friend works for the company in the USA Ravi replied.

e. Taj was very jealous Chandra agreed. But why would he steal it

f. I haven't lost it, Ravi retorted. I'm sure Taj took it   [6]

Reported speech is when you report what someone else has said. We do not use inverted commas in reported speech: *Chandra pointed out that Ravi always lost stuff.*

(2) Write the **reported speech** as **direct speech**.

Chandra said that Ravi didn't have any proof.

_____ [2]

(3) Write the **direct speech** as **reported speech**.

"What shall we do?" Ravi asked Taj.

_____ [2]

Paragraphs to organise ideas

> **Paragraphs** are sections in a long piece of writing. They group ideas together on the same theme. A new paragraph begins on a new line.

1 An alien spaceship landed in the playground at school. Your friends are describing what happened (see the speech bubbles), but in order to write a report you need to group similar ideas together into **three paragraphs**.

Decide which information should go in which paragraph, then write the correct letters under each heading. The first one has been done for you.

a. The alien came down on an escalator.

e. It had shiny metal on the outside.

h. It looked like a giant saucer.

b. It had three eyes on stalks.

f. The alien played football with the children.

c. It had blue lights around the side.

g. The spaceship landed on the football pitch.

i. The alien bowed and waved to the children.

d. It had a triangular head.

j. Its skin was furry.

The spaceship	What the alien looked like	What happened
		a

[9]

2 Create a suitable heading for your report.

_____ [1]

Adverbials and fronted adverbials

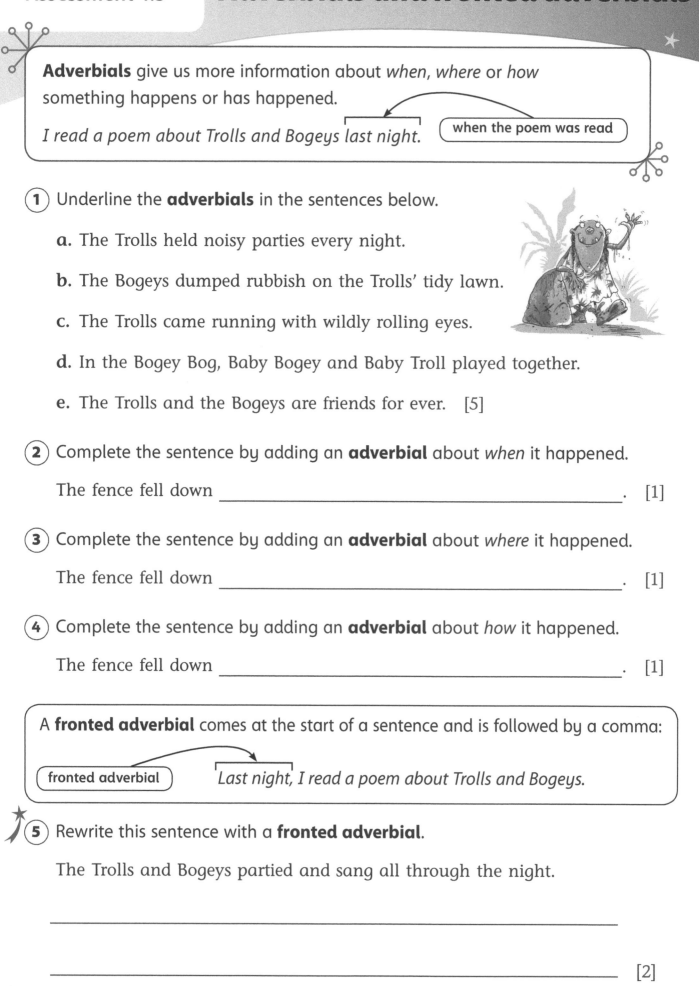

Adverbials give us more information about *when, where* or *how* something happens or has happened.

I read a poem about Trolls and Bogeys last night. (when the poem was read)

(**1**) Underline the **adverbials** in the sentences below.

  a. The Trolls held noisy parties every night.

  b. The Bogeys dumped rubbish on the Trolls' tidy lawn.

  c. The Trolls came running with wildly rolling eyes.

  d. In the Bogey Bog, Baby Bogey and Baby Troll played together.

  e. The Trolls and the Bogeys are friends for ever.   [5]

(**2**) Complete the sentence by adding an **adverbial** about *when* it happened.

The fence fell down _____. [1]

(**3**) Complete the sentence by adding an **adverbial** about *where* it happened.

The fence fell down _____. [1]

(**4**) Complete the sentence by adding an **adverbial** about *how* it happened.

The fence fell down _____. [1]

A **fronted adverbial** comes at the start of a sentence and is followed by a comma:

(fronted adverbial)   *Last night, I read a poem about Trolls and Bogeys.*

(**5**) Rewrite this sentence with a **fronted adverbial**.

The Trolls and Bogeys partied and sang all through the night.

_____

_____ [2]

Apostrophes for possession

An **apostrophe** is a mark like this ' that you use when something belongs to someone, e.g. *Tom's bike* (the bike that belongs to Tom) or *my friends' coats* (the coats that belong to my friends). It is called a **possessive apostrophe** because it shows who possesses (owns) something.

(1) Add a **possessive apostrophe** to the words underlined below.

   a. The <u>burglars</u> loot fell out of her sack.

   b. The <u>officers</u> notebook was in his pocket.

   c. It was the <u>criminals</u> fingerprints that gave her away.

   d. They knew he was guilty because they found the <u>thiefs</u> DNA.   [4]

Remember!

Singular means *one* of something. **Plural** means *more than one* of something. If the noun is singular, the apostrophe comes before the final s, e.g. *the teacher's coat* (one teacher). If the noun is plural, the apostrophe comes after the final s, e.g. *the teachers' coats* (more than one teacher).

(2) Circle the correct word in bold in each sentence.

   a. The **officer's/officers'** cars raced through the traffic lights.

   b. The **burglar's/burglars'** crimes were so bad that they were both sent to jail.

   c. Our **suspect's/suspects'** body language suggests they are all guilty.

   d. The detective was suspicious of **Matt's/Matts'** alibi.   [4]

If a *plural noun* does not end in an s, e.g. *men*, then an s is added, with an apostrophe before it, e.g. *the men's bikes.*

(3) Add a **possessive apostrophe** to the words underlined below.

   a. All the <u>childrens</u> pocket money has been stolen.

   b. The <u>womens</u> Olympic medals were stolen from the safe.   [2]

Standard English

Standard English is a way of speaking and writing that follows particular rules of grammar. In Standard English, the *subject* and *verb* should always agree.

I am joking. (Standard English)
I is joking. (non-Standard English)

(1) Tick **two** sentences that are written in **Standard English**.

We was late again. ☐

He was late again. ☐

I were just getting ready. ☐

They were just getting ready. ☐ [2]

(2) Circle the correct word in bold to complete each sentence in **Standard English**.

a. We **was/were** only asking for some more bread.

b. I **did/done** nothing wrong, Sir.

c. Some boys **is/are** very lazy nowadays.

d. I **am/be** freezing in this doorway, Hannah.

e. I **is/am** never going back to that workhouse.

f. **Them/Those** people were very kind to us. [6]

(3) Rewrite the sentence in **Standard English**.

All them poor kids was digging through the mud.

_____

_____ [2]

Grammar Assessment 4.6

Nouns and pronouns

> **Pronouns** can be used instead of **nouns**. Using a pronoun avoids repeating the noun again.
>
> (noun)   (pronoun)
>
> *Hamid picked up the tray of snacks and passed it*
> *under the windows of the departing bus.*

(1) Tick **two** statements that are correct.

A pronoun describes a verb. ☐

A pronoun can be used instead of a noun. ☐

A pronoun always comes before a noun. ☐

A pronoun avoids repeating the noun. ☐ [2]

(2) Circle the correct **pronoun** in bold in each sentence.

a. Hamid loved the bus station; **he/they** thought it was the best place in the world.

b. Passengers waved goodbye as **he/they** perched perilously on luggage racks.

c. Abba made sugarcane juice and sold **it/him** to customers.

d. On the cart were two painted eyes that looked like **them/they** held a secret.   [4]

(3) Circle the **pronoun** that refers to each underlined **noun**.

a. Salesmen clambered on board with their <u>goods</u>, clutching them tightly.

b. The <u>passengers</u> were grumpy but they watched Bulbul swallowing eggs.

c. The <u>bus</u> was ancient and it groaned and creaked.

d. One bold <u>man</u> stretched out and helped himself to a drink.   [4]

41

Expanded noun phrases

A **noun phrase** is a group of words with a noun as its 'head'. All the words in the phrase give more information about the noun. A noun phrase can be just two words:

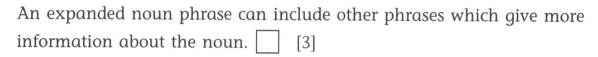

A noun phrase can also be **expanded**:

1 Tick **three** statements that are correct.

A noun phrase always has a verb in it. ☐

A noun phrase always has a noun in it. ☐

An expanded noun phrase means it is stretched across the page like elastic. ☐

An expanded noun phrase has more than one word describing the noun. ☐

An expanded noun phrase can include other phrases which give more information about the noun. ☐ [3]

2 Underline the **noun phrase** and circle the 'head' **noun** in each sentence.

a. We're a happy little family.

b. The baggy bogey frock belongs to Beryl.

c. This is our scruffy bogey dog. [6]

3 Rewrite the sentence, including an **expanded noun phrase**.

The Trolls held parties.

_____

_____ [1]

Determiners

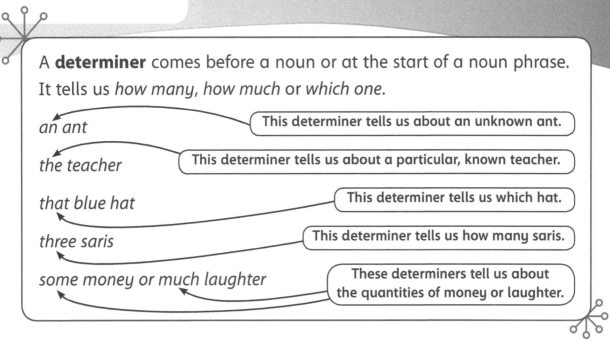

A **determiner** comes before a noun or at the start of a noun phrase. It tells us *how many*, *how much* or *which one*.

an ant — This determiner tells us about an unknown ant.

the teacher — This determiner tells us about a particular, known teacher.

that blue hat — This determiner tells us which hat.

three saris — This determiner tells us how many saris.

some money or much laughter — These determiners tell us about the quantities of money or laughter.

1 Tick **two** statements that are correct.

A determiner comes before a noun or at the start of a noun phrase. ☐

A determiner is used instead of a noun. ☐

A determiner can tell us how many, how much or which one. ☐

A determiner changes the meaning of a verb. ☐ [2]

2 Circle the **determiner** in each sentence.

a. Socks hang on the washing line.

b. That little orange jumper is mine.

c. It looked like an old cricket ball.

d. Many children ran out of school.

e. I saw five balloons, drifting like silken butterflies.

f. We found some hedgehogs curled up. [6]

3 Complete the sentence, using **two different determiners**.

I saw _____ birds sitting on _____ washing line. [2]

Possessive determiners

A **possessive determiner** tells you who something belongs to, e.g. *my, your, his, her, its, our, their.*

(1) Circle the **possessive determiner** in each sentence.

   a. We let our balloons float up to the turquoise skies.

   b. My kite dipped and drifted high in the sky.

   c. We had to chase your kite when the wind carried it away.

   d. Her sari has a mango leaf design.

   e. A girl dumps her bag and tiptoes forward.

   f. The hedgehog is curled up with its head tightly tucked in.   [6]

(2) Add a **possessive determiner** to each sentence.

   a. Girl, children, sky and sun hold _____ breath.

   b. The hedgehog stretched _____ legs and blinked.   [2]

(3) Tick **two** sentences that contain a **possessive determiner**.

   I left my school bag on the road. ☐

   That school bag on the road is mine. ☐

   I think that balloon is yours. ☐

   I think I can see your balloon. ☐   [2]

Possessive pronouns

A **possessive pronoun** tells you who something belongs to, e.g. *mine, yours, his, hers, ours, theirs.* It is used instead of a noun.

(1) Circle the **possessive pronoun** in each sentence.

   a. That little chick on the luggage rack is mine!

   b. Hamid asked the passengers if the money he found was theirs.

   c. My sugarcane juice is sweeter than hers.

   d. Leave that cart alone – it's ours! [4]

(2) Add a **possessive pronoun** to each sentence.

   a. Abba gave the man and his son a glass of sugarcane juice each and said, "These are _____."

   b. Abba told Hamid that the money he made that day was _____ to keep.

   c. A woman grabbed the bag that she thought was _____.

   d. I was sitting in that seat earlier – it's _____. [4]

(3) Tick **two** sentences that contain a **possessive pronoun**.

   My daughter recognises the bracelet – it's hers. ☐

   My daughter knows the bracelet belongs to her. ☐

   I gave Bulbul the handkerchief he had dropped and said, "This is yours." ☐

   I gave Bulbul the handkerchief he had dropped and said, "This is your handkerchief." ☐ [2]

Grammar Assessment 4.1 **Punctuating speech**

(1) Award 1 mark for each sentence punctuated correctly.

    a. "I've got an idea**,"** Chandra said thoughtfully.

    b. "Taj, I've got something to show you**,"** Ravi said.

    c. Ravi whispered to Chandra, **"**What's Mum talking about? Taj gets everything he wants.**"**

    d. "Our dad's friend works for a company in the USA**,"** Ravi replied.

    e. "Taj was very jealous**,"** Chandra agreed. "But why would he steal it?"

    f. "I haven't lost it," Ravi retorted. "I'm sure Taj took it.**"** **[6]**

(2) Award 1 mark for insertion of (double or single) inverted commas and **1 mark** for punctuation within the inverted commas, e.g.

"You don't have any proof Ravi," Chandra said. **[2]**

(3) Award 1 mark for writing the correct words and **1 mark** for correct punctuation.

Ravi asked Taj what they should do. **[2]**

Grammar Assessment 4.2 **Paragraphs to organise ideas**

(1) Award 1 mark for each letter listed under the correct heading

The spaceship	What the alien looked like	What happened
		a
c	b	f
e	d	g
h	j	i [9]

(2) Award 1 mark for a suitable heading that is related to the topic, e.g.

Alien landing on football pitch **[1]**

Grammar Assessment 4.3 **Adverbials and fronted adverbials**

(1) **Award 1 mark** for each adverbial identified.

a. The Trolls held noisy parties **every night**.

b. The Bogeys dumped rubbish **on the Trolls' tidy lawn**.

c. The Trolls came running **with wildly rolling eyes**.

d. **In the Bogey Bog**, Baby Bogey and Baby Troll played together.

e. The Trolls and the Bogeys are friends **for ever**. **[5]**

(2) **Award 1 mark** for adding a plausible adverbial about *when* the fence fell down, e.g. The fence fell down **last night**. **[1]**

(3) **Award 1 mark** for adding a plausible adverbial about *where* the fence fell down, e.g. The fence fell down **in the back garden**. **[1]**

(4) **Award 1 mark** for adding a plausible adverbial about *how* the fence fell down, e.g. The fence fell down **with a loud crash**. **[1]**

(5) **Award 1 mark** for positioning the adverbial at the beginning of the sentence and **1 mark** for inserting a comma after it.

All through the night, the Trolls and Bogeys partied and sang. **[2]**

Grammar Assessment 4.4 **Apostrophes for possession**

(1) **Award 1 mark** for each apostrophe inserted in the correct position.

a. The burglar**'s** loot fell out of her sack.

b. The officer**'s** notebook was in his pocket.

c. It was the criminal**'s** fingerprints that gave her away.

d. They knew he was guilty because they found the thief**'s** DNA. **[4]**

(2) **Award 1 mark** for each correct word.

a. The **officer's**/officers' cars raced through the traffic lights.

b. The **burglar's**/burglars' crimes were so bad that they were both sent to jail.

c. Our **suspect's**/suspects' body language suggests they are all guilty.

d. The detective was suspicious of Matt's/**Matts'** alibi. **[4]**

(3) **Award 1 mark** for each apostrophe inserted in the correct position.

a. All the children**'s** pocket money has been stolen.

b. The women**'s** Olympic medals were stolen from the safe. **[2]**

Grammar Assessment 4.5 **Standard English**

(1) **Award 1 mark** for each correct box ticked.

We was late again. ☐

He was late again. ☑

I were just getting ready. ☐

They were just getting ready. ☑   **[2]**

(2) **Award 1 mark** for each correct word.

a. We **was/(were)** only asking for some more bread.

b. I **(did)/done** nothing wrong, Sir.

c. Some boys **is/(are)** very lazy nowadays.

d. I **(am)/be** freezing in this doorway, Hannah.

e. I **is/(am)** never going back to that workhouse.

f. **Them/(Those)** people were very kind to us.   **[6]**

(3) **Award 1 mark** for correctly substituting 'them' and **1 mark** for correctly substituting 'was'.

All **those** poor kids **were** digging through the mud.   **[2]**

Grammar Assessment 4.6 **Nouns and pronouns**

(1) **Award 1 mark** for each correct box ticked.

A pronoun describes a verb. ☐

A pronoun can be used instead of a noun. ☑

A pronoun always comes before a noun. ☐

A pronoun avoids repeating the noun. ☑   **[2]**

(2) **Award 1 mark** for each correct word.

a. Hamid loved the bus station; **(he)/they** thought it was the best place in the world.

b. Passengers waved goodbye as **he/(they)** perched perilously on luggage racks.

c. Abba made sugarcane juice and sold **(it)/him** to customers.

d. On the cart were two painted eyes that looked like **them/(they)** held a secret.   **[4]**

(3) **Award 1 mark** for each correct word.

a. Salesmen clambered on board with their goods, clutching **(them)** tightly.

b. The passengers were grumpy but **(they)** watched Bulbul swallowing eggs.

c. The bus was ancient and **(it)** groaned and creaked.

d. One bold man stretched out and helped **(himself)** to a drink.   **[4]**

Grammar Assessment 4.7 **Expanded noun phrases**

(**1**) **Award 1 mark** for each correct box ticked.

A noun phrase always has a verb in it. ☐

A noun phrase always has a noun in it. ☑

An expanded noun phrase means it is stretched across the page like elastic. ☐

An expanded noun phrase has more than one word describing the noun. ☑

An expanded noun phrase can include other phrases which give more information

about the noun. ☑ **[3]**

(**2**) **Award 1 mark** for each noun phrase identified and **1 mark** for each 'head' noun identified.

a. We're a <u>happy little (family)</u>.

b. The <u>baggy bogey (frock)</u> belongs to Beryl.

c. This is our <u>scruffy bogey (dog)</u>. **[6]**

(**3**) **Award 1 mark** for an example of an expanded noun phrase, e.g.

The Trolls held noisy parties in their garden. **[1]**

Grammar Assessment 4.8 **Determiners**

(**1**) **Award 1 mark** for each correct box ticked.

A determiner comes before a noun or at the start of a noun phrase. ☑

A determiner is used instead of a noun. ☐

A determiner can tell us how many, how much or which one. ☑

A determiner changes the meaning of a verb. ☐ **[2]**

(**2**) **Award 1 mark** for each determiner identified.

a. Socks hang on (the) washing line.

b. (That) little orange jumper is mine.

c. It looked like (an) old cricket ball.

d. (Many) children ran out of school.

e. I saw (five) balloons, drifting like silken butterflies.

f. We found (some) hedgehogs curled up. **[6]**

(**3**) **Award 1 mark** for each plausible determiner inserted, e.g.

I saw **some** birds sitting on **the** washing line.

I saw **three** birds sitting on **a** washing line.

I saw **the** birds sitting on **that** washing line. **[2]**

Grammar Assessment 4.9 **Possessive determiners**

(1) **Award 1 mark** for each possessive determiner identified.

  a. We let (our) balloons float up to the turquoise skies.

  b. (My) kite dipped and drifted high in the sky.

  c. We had to chase (your) kite when the wind carried it away.

  d. (Her) sari has a mango leaf design.

  e. A girl dumps (her) bag and tiptoes forward.

  f. The hedgehog is curled up with (its) head tightly tucked in. **[6]**

(2) **Award 1 mark** for each plausible possessive determiner inserted, e.g.

  a. Girl, children, sky and sun hold **their** breath.

  b. The hedgehog stretched **its/his/her** legs and blinked. **[2]**

(3) **Award 1 mark** for each correct box ticked.

  I left my school bag on the road. ☑   I think that balloon is yours. ☐

  That school bag on the road is mine. ☐ I think I can see your balloon. ☑ **[2]**

Grammar Assessment 4.10 **Possessive pronouns**

(1) **Award 1 mark** for each possessive pronoun identified.

  a. That little chick on the luggage rack is (mine)!

  b. Hamid asked the passengers if the money he found was (theirs).

  c. My sugarcane juice is sweeter than (hers).

  d. Leave that cart alone – it's (ours)! **[4]**

(2) **Award 1 mark** for each correct possessive pronoun inserted.

  a. Abba gave the man and his son a glass of sugarcane juice each and said,
    "These are **yours**."

  b. Abba told Hamid that the money he made that day was **his** to keep.

  c. A woman grabbed the bag she thought was **hers**.

  d. I was sitting in that seat earlier – it's **mine**. **[4]**

(3) **Award 1 mark** for each correct box ticked.

  My daughter recognises the bracelet – it's hers. ☑

  My daughter knows the bracelet belongs to her. ☐

  I gave Bulbul the handkerchief her had dropped and said, "This is yours." ☑

  I gave Bulbul the handkerchief he had dropped and said, "This is your
  handkerchief." ☐ **[2]**

End of Year Grammar Test 4

1 Tick the sentence that has the correct punctuation.

The teacher shouted "Come back!" ☐

The teacher shouted "Come back"! ☐

The teacher shouted, "Come back!" ☐ [1]

2 Add the correct punctuation to the sentence below.

What is your name asked Jamila. [3]

3 Underline the **adverbial** in the sentence below.

Please choose a book before you leave. [1]

4 Rewrite the sentence below so that it begins with the **adverbial**. Use only the same words, and remember to punctuate your answer correctly.

Rob ate the cake greedily. [2]

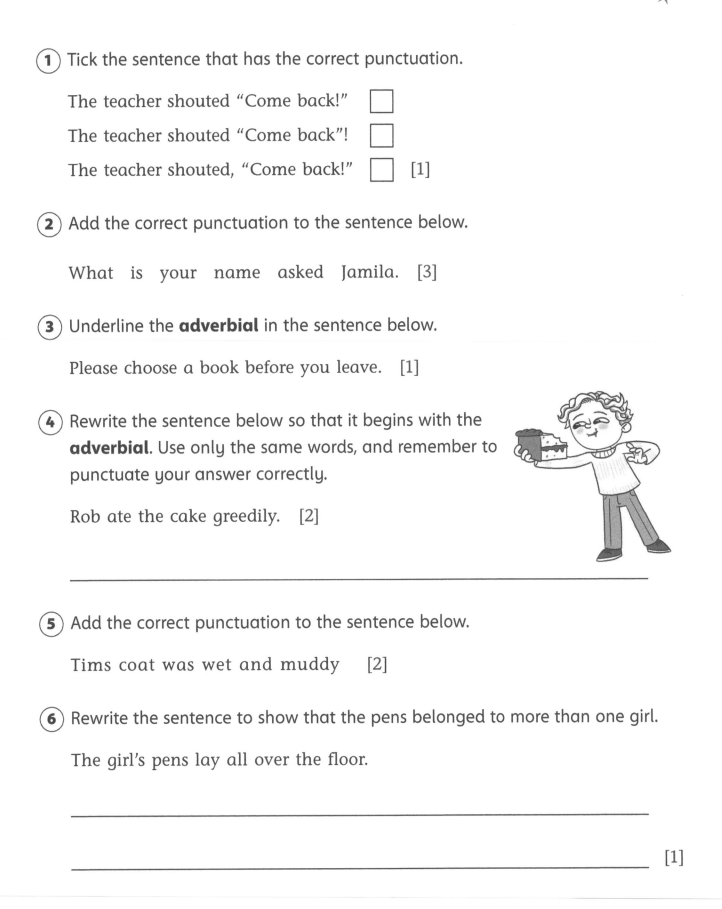

_____

5 Add the correct punctuation to the sentence below.

Tims coat was wet and muddy [2]

6 Rewrite the sentence to show that the pens belonged to more than one girl.

The girl's pens lay all over the floor.

_____

_____ [1]

(7) Tick the two sentences that use **Standard English**.

We was looking at the birds in the trees. ☐

We were taking presents to the party. ☐

I do like swimming in the sea. ☐

I done more chores than you. ☐ [2]

(8) Tick the **noun** that the **pronoun** 'it' replaces.

The wind slammed the door shut. <u>It</u> made the windows rattle in their frames.

wind ☐ door ☐ windows ☐ [1]

(9) The words below are an **expanded noun phrase**.

the pale girl with freckles

Turn the noun phrase below into an **expanded noun phrase.**

the cat _____ [2]

(10) Circle **three determiners** in the sentence below.

I found some cobwebs under the bed, so I knew a spider had been there. [3]

(11) Tick the correct **word class** of the word 'my' in this sentence.

I left <u>my</u> homework in the kitchen.

verb ☐ noun ☐ determiner ☐ [1]

(12) Circle the **possessive pronoun** in the sentence below.

That cute little puppy is hers. [1]

TOTAL MARKS: _____ / 20

1 Award **1 mark** for the correct box ticked.

The teacher shouted "Come back!" ☐

The teacher shouted "Come back"! ☐

The teacher shouted, "Come back!" ✓ **[1]**

2 Award **1 mark** for a question mark and **1 mark** for each inverted comma (double or single).

"What is your name**?**" asked Jamila. **[3]**

3 Award **1 mark** for identifying the adverbial.

Please choose a book <u>before you leave</u>. **[1]**

4 Award **1 mark** for moving the adverbial to the beginning of the sentence, and **1 mark** for inserting a comma after the adverbial.

Greedily, Rob ate the cake. **[2]**

5 Award **1 mark** for each correct piece of punctuation.

Tim's coat was wet and muddy**.** **[2]**

6 Award **1 mark** for inserting the apostrophe in the correct place.

The girls' pens lay all over the floor. **[1]**

7 Award **1 mark** for each correct box ticked.

We was looking at the birds in the trees. ☐   I do like swimming in the sea. ✓

We were taking presents to the party. ✓   I done more chores than you. ☐ **[2]**

8 Award **1 mark** for the correct box ticked.

wind ✓   door ☐   windows ☐ **[1]**

9 Award **2 marks** for a complete expanded noun phrase, e.g.

the cat **with the fluffy tail** **[2]**

10 Award **1 mark** for each determiner identified.

I found (some) cobwebs under (the) bed, so I knew (a) spider had been there. **[3]**

11 Award **1 mark** for the correct box ticked.

verb ☐   noun ☐   determiner ✓ **[1]**

12 Award **1 mark** for identifying the possessive pronoun.

That cute little puppy is (hers). **[1]**

Reading Assessments

Introduction

Introduce the task

Show your enthusiasm for the text children are about to read, and make links to their work in *Literacy and Language* to engage their interest.

Timing

Explain to the children that they will have 30 minutes to complete the task. You may wish to suggest that they spend 10 minutes reading and 20 minutes answering the questions.

Completing the task

Ask children to complete the task quietly and independently. Do monitor children, however, and support children who need help.

Should all children complete the task?

These assessments are intended to be used with children who are reading fluently (above the equivalent of National Curriculum Level 2a) and who have completed the relevant *Literacy and Language* unit. Do not ask children to begin the task if you feel it will be too challenging for them, or prolong the task if children are obviously struggling.

Marking the task

The Mark Schemes are provided to give an indication of how to mark the Reading Assessment Question Papers. Each Reading Assessment Question Paper has 15 available marks. The Reading Assessment Question Papers enable you to check and monitor children's progress in reading comprehension using the Assessment Progress Trackers available online (see the 'Teaching and Assessment' resources for *Read Write Inc.* on www.oxfordowl.co.uk).

The National Curriculum Tests will be given a 'scaled score', so at the time of publication there is not a defined pass mark that children must achieve.

Award half marks or part of the mark allocation for a question at your discretion – these tests are designed to enable you to track your children's progress in the key assessable reading skills they will need to demonstrate for the National Curriculum Tests. Using the online Assessment Progress Trackers, you can identify which assessable skills children are confident with, and which might need extra practice. Further information about assessment and levelling will be given on www.oxfordowl.co.uk as it becomes available.

The question formats in the Reading Assessment Question Papers draw on those used in the National Curriculum Tests, to familiarise children with them. The mark allocation usually matches that in the National Curriculum Tests sample mark schemes, to signal the length of explanation that children need to give. In places, different numbers of marks are awarded to questions with a similar format, where they present varying levels of challenge.

The most stretching questions are marked with a shooting star, to indicate that these are challenge questions which children must think especially carefully about.

Tracking progress

Assessment Progress Trackers are provided online which map the curriculum objectives for reading to the questions on the Reading Assessment Question Papers, to allow you to identify areas in which children are confident, or may need further practice.

This will be matched to the government assessment system when more information about this is available. See the 'Teaching and Assessment' area for *Read Write Inc.* on www.oxfordowl.co.uk for updates.

These Reading Assessments aim to prepare children gradually for the National Curriculum Tests, in shorter practice sessions. To check children's reading stamina when encountering a number of texts, complete the Practice Assessment Papers online (in the 'Teaching and Assessment' area for *Read Write Inc.*) which closely match the format of the End of Key Stage National Curriculum Tests.

Useful words

See below for some useful words that you may wish to explain to children before they begin each Reading Assessment.

Reading Assessment 3.1
The Fish in Room 11

promenade	venture
gangplank	encrusted
stocking	swilling

Reading Assessment 3.2
Unusual Hobbies

You may wish to select your own useful words from this text, depending on the needs of your children.

Reading Assessment 3.3
Dinosaur Pox

scaly	smirked
snout	buds
triumphantly	sniggered

Reading Assessment 3.4
How Do Submarines Work?

ballast	compartment
vessel	hatch
valves	

Reading Assessment 3.5
About Knees

ointment

Reading Assessment 3.6
Akimbo and the Lions

wart hogs
earmarked
marauding

Reading Assessment 4.1
The Demon Headmaster

waver	woodenly
earnest	unison
gabbled	

Reading Assessment 4.2
Dear Mum

waste-disposal unit

Reading Assessment 4.3
The Beastman of Ballyloch

hauling	limp
clutching	repellent

Reading Assessment 4.4
Save the Elephants of Vietnam

extinction	vulnerable
ivory	endangered
ornaments	bleaker
timber	dwindling

Reading Assessment 4.5
Cloud Tea Monkeys

plantation
overseer

Reading Assessment 4.6
Coming to England

wares	cascading
intoxicating	awash
unceremoniously	wharf

The Fish in Room 11

Heather Dyer

Toby lives in a hotel at the seaside. Cook has woken him up to complain that her washing has blown away in a storm and it's Toby's fault because he forgot to bring it in. In this part of the story, Toby sets off to look for the washing.

Toby stood in front of the hotel. There was a playful wind blowing after the storm and a paper bag and a few chocolate wrappers swirled past like autumn leaves. It was an exciting wind – the sort of wind that seems to have come from a long way away and brings surprises. It was the sort of day, thought Toby, when you might find a shipwrecked sailor lying on the sand, or a message in a green bottle.

The beach was deserted and the pier was closed. The shutters were down on the souvenir kiosks and were rattling in the wind, and the metal claw hung poised over the tank of stuffed toys in the arcade. Apart from an old lady and her small dog on the promenade, Toby was the only one about.

But things would soon be different – it was Cake Day. In less than an hour the ship would arrive. Passengers would pour down the gangplank and along the pier and into The Grand for tea and cakes. This reminded Toby that Cook was waiting impatiently for her lost laundry, and he set off in search of it.

Straight away he spotted a wet tea towel clumped on the ground, then he found a tablecloth flapping from the railings and a face cloth in the gutter. He gathered them up and hurried down the ramp to the beach and there he came across Cook's apron, a second tea towel and the other red stocking, all covered with sand. But where was Cook's cap? Toby walked the whole length of the beach and back again but Cook's cap was nowhere to be seen. There was one place however, where Toby still hadn't looked, so he left the bundle of washing on the sand and stepped bravely into the shadows of the pier.

People didn't usually venture under the pier; it was chilly and damp and the water rose and fell restlessly around black, mussel-encrusted pillars. Toby shivered. There was no sign of the cap – just the darkly swilling sea.

But just as he was about to turn back Toby heard a noise – a sharp, cracking noise. Then it stopped.

'Hello?' he called.

There was no reply but the wash of the waves. Toby turned to go but then the noise came again – nearer this time. It sounded just like someone cracking nuts. And what was that? Was someone moving out there between the pillars?

'Hello?' called Toby in a shrill voice. 'Who's there?'

For a moment there was no reply, then all of a sudden a girl's pale face peeped out from behind a pillar – and she was wearing Cook's cap! Keeping her eye on Toby, the girl cracked a mussel with her back teeth and ate the meat as though it was a nut.

'Er…that's Cook's cap,' said Toby.

'It is?' said the girl.

'Yes.'

The girl tutted. 'All right then,' she said, and the next moment she had left the pillar and was moving swiftly through the water towards Toby. But she was not swimming, she was *gliding* through the water with her arms at her sides and a little wave cresting before her.

The Fish in Room 11

(1) a) **Look at the first paragraph. What is the weather like? Tick one.**

very rainy ☐   windy ☐   hot and sunny ☐   foggy ☐

[1 mark]

b) **How does the weather make Toby feel? Tick one.**

bored and frustrated ☐   sad ☐
excited and expectant ☐   angry ☐

[1 mark]

(2) **Find and copy a word that shows what it is like on the beach.**

_____

[1 mark]

(3) **Which of these things happen in the first two paragraphs? Tick one.**

Toby finds a message in a bottle. ☐   Toby eats lots of cake. ☐
Toby sunbathes. ☐   Toby sets off to look for the lost washing. ☐

[1 mark]

(4) **Number the items in the order Toby finds them. The first one has been done for you.**

Cook's cap ___

a tablecloth ___

a wet tea towel _1_

Cook's apron, a second tea towel and the red stocking ___

[1 mark]

(5) a) *The beach was deserted…*

The word *deserted* means… (Tick one.)

busy ☐   loud ☐   empty ☐   full ☐

[1 mark]

b) *...Cook was waiting impatiently...*

Cook is feeling... (Tick one.)

happy ☐ bored and angry ☐ excited ☐ sad and lonely ☐

[1 mark]

⑥ **Find** and **copy two** words that describe what it is like under the pier.

_____

[2 marks]

⑦ Why does Toby stop as he is about to leave the pier?

_____

[1 mark]

⑧ How do you think Toby feels when he meets the girl under the pier? Use evidence from the text to support your answer.

_____

_____

_____

[3 marks]

⑨ Based on what you have read, what do you think might happen next? Use the text to support your answer.

_____

_____

_____

[2 marks]

Unusual Hobbies

Everybody gets some free time, right? Your school may be mean enough to give you masses of homework each night. Your parents might make you do chores at home: "Wash the dishes!" "Tidy your room!" (Surely parents were invented to do that sort of thing?) But everybody gets at least *some* free time. How do you spend yours?

You've probably got some kind of hobby ...

Collectors

Coins, dolls, autographs, stamps, shells, plastic toys, football cards – they're all great things to collect.

But maybe you could think a bit more creatively. Believe it or not, there are children out there who have collections of: bottle tops; felt-tip pen lids (not the pens, just the lids!); sweet wrappers; snails (yuk!); even those little packets of ketchup that they give you in fast-food restaurants.
Could you start a collection that nobody's ever thought of before?

Can you believe it? An Australian man has been collecting his own belly button fluff since 1984. He's got three jars full of it. Seriously!

Crafters

It's great to recycle things that would normally be thrown away, and make models from them. Lots of you probably do it already. Maybe you could go a step further…

If you're really careful, you can carve fantastic shapes from bars of soap. Draw the outline with a pencil, then scrape the soap away around it, bit by bit, to create your shape. You might start with something simple, like a fish. The greatest carvers can produce flowers, or even lifelike human faces.

For a two-in-one hobby, you could even make your own musical instruments to play. Drums, shakers, thumb pianos and xylophones can all be built from things you can find around the house.

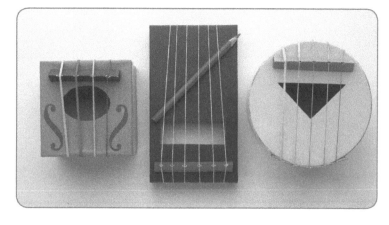

Why not make a band with your brothers, sisters or friends? Remember: the louder the better, to really annoy your parents!

Adventurers

Sports and outdoor activities are fantastic hobbies because they get you out of the house and help to keep you fit. Football, tennis, rugby, swimming, cycling and athletics are wonderful sports to get involved in.

If you happen to live close to the sea, why not try surfing or bodyboarding? They're both really fun and great for fitness. Remember: the sea is dangerous, so get lessons from the surf school experts, or ask your parents to teach you. And don't forget to slap on that sun cream!

For you city kids, make use of your local stunt bike or skateboard tracks. Racing or practising stunts with your friends can be a fantastic way to spend your free time. But safety comes first! Always strap on padding and a helmet before attempting any moves.

Love them or hate them, you can't deny that roller coaster rides can be a real thrill. But surely there's a limit to how many you can cope with? Not for some people. They just can't stay off them! There are people who have ridden over 1,000 different roller coasters around the world. One 78-year-old American man even went on the same roller coaster 90 times in a day. Definitely not a hobby for those of you with weak tummies!

Unusual Hobbies

1 Which items does the writer think are great things to collect? Tick **two**.

sweets ☐   shells ☐   coins ☐   sticks ☐

[2 marks]

2 Which less usual items does the writer say that children collect?
Tick **two**.

envelopes ☐   pen lids ☐   leaves ☐   ketchup packets ☐

[2 marks]

3 *It's great to recycle things…*

The word *recycle* means… (Tick **one**.)

paint ☐   use again ☐   store ☐   talk to ☐

[1 mark]

4 The writer tells us about an unusual material that can be used to make
shapes, such as a fish or flowers. What is it?

_____

[1 mark]

5 Give **two** sports and outdoor activities that the writer suggests.

_____

[1 mark]

6 How many times did the 78-year-old American ride a roller coaster in
one day?

_____

[1 mark]

7 Why should you get proper lessons if you learn to surf or bodyboard?

_____

[1 mark]

(8) Look at the subheading 'Adventurers'. Which of the following could replace this subheading? Tick **one**.

Other indoor activities ☐   Outdoor activities ☐

Shopping and leisure ☐   Dance and drama ☐

[1 mark]

(9) a) What does the writer suggest that city kids do?

_____

[1 mark]

b) Why does the writer advise the reader to strap on padded gear?

_____

[1 mark]

(10) *How do you spend yours?*

Why do you think the writer asks questions in the text?

_____

_____

[1 mark]

(11) a) What is the purpose of this text? Tick **one**.

to **argue** ☐   to **persuade** ☐   to **inform** ☐   to **tell a story** ☐

[1 mark]

b) Who do you think the text has been written for?

_____

[1 mark]

Dinosaur Pox

Jeremy Strong

Jodie is fed up. She doesn't like her hair, her freckles or her little brother, Mark. He says that if she stares at her scary face in the mirror too long, she'll turn into stone. But in this part of the story, we find out that Jodie doesn't turn into stone – she turns into something else.

That night something unusual happened. In fact it was more than unusual – it was extraordinary, incredible, fantastic, mind-boggling and bizarre – and it happened to Jodie.

Nobody knew how it happened, or why it happened. All they knew was that when Jodie went to bed she was herself – in other words, grumpy – but when Jodie woke up the next morning she had changed. She wasn't Jodie any longer.

She was a dinosaur.

It was a dinosaur that got out of bed the next day – a dinosaur with fat, stumpy legs like thick tree trunks. Instead of freckles, she had purple and green blotches all over her fat, scaly body. She had a long thick tail. She had great leathery plates sticking out of her back, like fins that had been designed by somebody who couldn't draw. She had a small head with little red glinting eyes, a long snout, and an even longer thick purple tongue.

Jodie knew something was wrong the moment she woke up. She struggled across to her mirror.

'Oh, isn't that just great,' she muttered. 'I'm a dinosaur. Just my luck. Why does nothing nice ever happen to me? First I'm given freckles and horrible hair, and now I've turned into a dinosaur.'

She suddenly had a thought. Maybe she *had* stared at herself in the mirror too long, just like Mark said.

Jodie trotted across to Mark's room and pushed open his door with her snout. 'You were wrong,' she announced triumphantly. 'I haven't turned into stone. I've turned into a dinosaur, so there.'

Mark took one look at his sister and his jaw dropped. 'Wow!' he breathed. 'That is incredible! How did you do it? Can I do it too?' He fished around in a box beneath his bed and pulled out a plastic dinosaur. 'You're just like this model. You're a stegosaurus.'

Jodie was secretly pleased that, just for once, she had managed to impress her brother, but Mr and Mrs Bolton were not impressed at all.

'How long are you going to stay like that?' asked Dad. 'You've got school in fifteen minutes.'

'Everyone will laugh at me,' complained Jodie.

'They laugh at you anyway,' smirked Mark. 'Shall I put your cereal on the floor, or are you going to sit up at the table?'

'Don't tease,' said Mum, putting Jodie's bowl on the kitchen floor.

'I don't want it anyway,' grumbled Jodie.

'You must eat something.'

'I expect she wants plants,' said Mark. 'Stegosauruses were plant eaters.'

Jodie hated to admit it, but Mark was right. She did fancy some plants.

'It's because you're a vegetarian,' Mark claimed. 'Eating all those vegetables has turned you into a dinosaur.'

Mrs Bolton let Jodie out into the back garden and watched as her daughter wandered round the flower beds chewing bushes and nibbling at tender buds. 'Oh dear, I rather liked those big white daisies, but Jodie seems to like them too.'

When Dad left for work, he decided he ought to make an appointment for Jodie at the doctor's surgery. 'I've never heard of a child turning into a dinosaur before, but maybe the doctor has. I'm sure Jodie will be back to normal soon.'

'Jodie? Normal?' sniggered Mark. 'That's impossible.'

Dad's face clouded. He was worried that Mark was quite probably right. On the other hand, he didn't really fancy bringing up a dinosaur in the family.

Dinosaur Pox

1 **What is Jodie like when she is her usual self? Tick one.**

happy ☐   grumpy ☐   popular ☐   calm ☐

[1 mark]

2 **Why does the narrator say that Jodie turned into a dinosaur? Tick one.**

Nobody knows. ☐   She ate too many vegetables. ☐

She looked in the mirror. ☐   She teased her brother. ☐

[1 mark]

3 **What does Jodie dislike about her usual appearance? Find two things.**

_____

[1 mark]

4 **a) How does Mark feel when he realises Jodie has turned into a dinosaur? Tick one.**

He is impressed. ☐   He is scared. ☐

He is sad. ☐   He is angry. ☐

[1 mark]

b) Find and copy a word or phrase in the text that shows how Mark feels.

_____

[1 mark]

5 **Match up the synonyms from the story.**

complained	incredible
chewing	grumbled
extraordinary	nibbling

[3 marks]

(6) **What does Jodie eat when she is a dinosaur? Tick one.**

meat ☐   daisies ☐   insects ☐   cereal ☐

[1 mark]

(7) a) **How does Mark treat Jodie in this part of the story? Tick one.**

He comforts her. ☐   He chases her. ☐
He teases her. ☐   He runs away from her. ☐

[1 mark]

b) **Find** and **copy** a phrase from the story that shows this.

_____

[1 mark]

(8) **On page 71, what reason does Mark give for Jodie becoming a dinosaur?**

She ate too much meat. ☐   She ate too many vegetables. ☐
She read too much. ☐   She was rude to her mum. ☐

[1 mark]

(9) **Using the story, tick one box in each row to show whether each statement is true or false.**

	True	False
Mum runs away because she is frightened.		
Dad plans to take Jodie to the doctor.		

[1 mark]

(10) **Why do you think Jodie's family react in the way they do when Jodie turns into a dinosaur? Use the text to support your answer.**

_____

_____

[2 marks]

How Do Submarines Work?

A submarine, like a ship, is just a very large metal container that can hold lots of people and equipment.

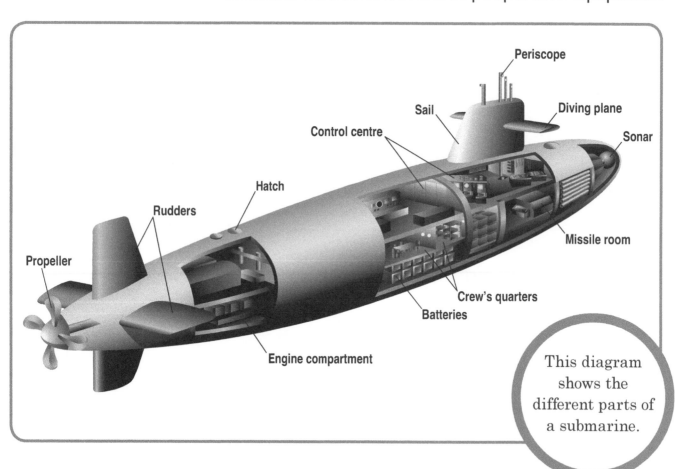

Periscope

Sail

Diving plane

Control centre

Sonar

Hatch

Rudders

Missile room

Propeller

Crew's quarters

Batteries

Engine compartment

This diagram shows the different parts of a submarine.

What makes it special is that it can dive under the waves to move about without being seen. This is really important, especially during wartime. A sub can prowl around the deep ocean like a hidden cat waiting to pounce.

Controlling the submarine

Submarines have huge containers on their sides that can be filled with air or water. They are called 'ballast tanks'. When the sub is on the surface, these tanks are filled with air. This makes the vessel light, so it floats. When it's time to dive under the surface, valves are opened to let some water into the ballast tanks, forcing some of the air out. As a result, the sub becomes heavier and it starts to sink.

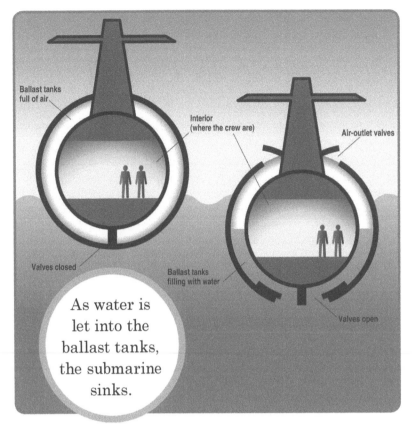

Ballast tanks full of air

Interior (where the crew are)

Air-outlet valves

Valves closed

Ballast tanks filling with water

Valves open

As water is let into the ballast tanks, the submarine sinks.

Once the commanding officer has got the sub down to the right depth, he needs to pump a little more air into the ballast tanks so the sub stops sinking. He has to balance the water and air mix so that the sub is exactly the right weight to float below the waves. When the commanding officer wants to surface again, all he has to do is give the order to pump more air into the ballast tanks and let some water out.

This submarine is diving down through the water.

A life underwater

Modern submarines could stay underwater for years at a time – if there was enough food on board. It's not an easy life for the crew, though. There's obviously no sunlight, and no contact with friends or family is allowed – sending a text or making a phone call could give away the sub's position.

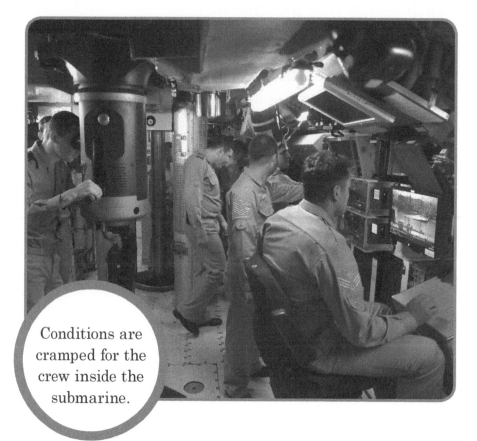

Conditions are cramped for the crew inside the submarine.

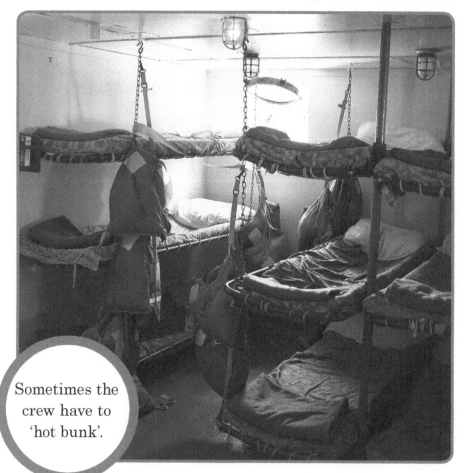

Sometimes the crew have to 'hot bunk'.

There's not much room to move and no chance for the crew to have any time to themselves. It can get very hot, very sticky and very smelly. (The crew are not even allowed to use body sprays!)

The crew usually work for six hours at a time, and sleep when they're not working. Sometimes they have to 'hot bunk' – that means when one man gets out of his bunk bed to start work, another jumps straight into it to sleep!

As well as being used during wartime, submarines can be used by scientists for research, or as 'tourist submarines' for underwater safaris.

The crew can see lots of different types of fish from the submarine portholes.

Escaping from a submarine

In an emergency, it's possible to escape from a damaged submarine. The crew member must first put on a special suit. This will protect him from the cold and water pressure. He then goes into a sealed compartment. A hatch is opened and the crew member escapes into the water, travelling upwards at 2–3 metres per second. The suit contains an inflatable life raft for when he reaches the surface.

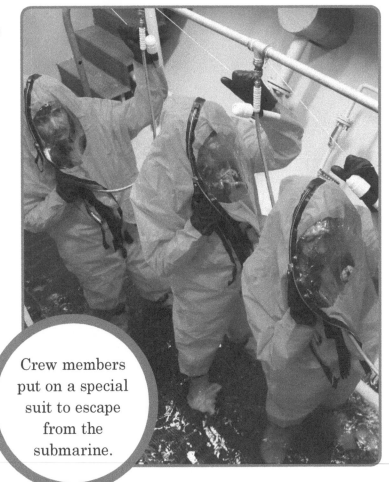

Crew members put on a special suit to escape from the submarine.

77

How Do Submarines Work?

① **What is special about a submarine? Tick one.**

It is very big. ☐   It can dive underwater. ☐

It is very heavy. ☐   It glows in the dark. ☐

[1 mark]

② **What are the containers on the sides of the submarine called? Tick one.**

vessels ☐   subs ☐   valves ☐   ballast tanks ☐

[1 mark]

③ **Is a submarine useful during wartime? Give a reason for your answer.**

_____

_____

[2 marks]

④ **What happens to make the submarine dive underwater? Tick one.**

It folds up. ☐

It becomes invisible. ☐

Air fills the ballast tanks to makes the submarine lighter. ☐

Water fills the ballast tanks to make the submarine heavier. ☐

[1 mark]

⑤ **What title is given to the person in charge of the submarine? Tick one.**

captain ☐   chief ☐   commanding officer ☐   crew head ☐

[1 mark]

⑥ **How long can modern submarines stay underwater?**

_____

[1 mark]

(7) **a) What is the purpose of this text? Tick one.**

to **argue** ☐ to **persuade** ☐ to **explain** ☐ to **tell a story** ☐

[1 mark]

b) Give a reason for your answer.

_____

[1 mark]

(8) How do crew members escape from a submarine in an emergency? Explain using your own words.

_____

_____

_____

[2 marks]

(9) Using the text, tick one box in each row to show whether each statement is a **fact** or an **opinion**. The first one has been done for you.

	Fact	Opinion
Submarines are really exciting!		✓
There is very little space inside a submarine so it can get very hot.		
It would be fantastic to live on a submarine.		

[2 marks]

(10) The text explains that it can be hard living on a submarine. Give **two** reasons why.

_____

_____

_____

[2 marks]

About Knees

Mum doesn't understand about knees,
how they need a smear of mud
to look cool in the playground.
She scrubs them with a flannel.

Mum doesn't understand about knees,
how they always stick out,
and they graze when you fall over.
She fixes plasters across them.

Mum doesn't understand about knees,
how they get the best bruises –
all purple and yellow blotches.
She rubs greasy ointment into them.

Mum doesn't understand about knees,
how they're just right for drawing
beetles on with a green felt tip.
She takes the nail brush to them.

Perhaps Mum should wear shorts next summer,
see what happens to HER knees.
And I'll be ready with the flannel,
the plasters, ointment and nail brush.

Alison Chisholm

About Knees

(1) **What does the poet say makes knees look cool in the playground?**
Tick one.

a sticker ☐   a smear of mud ☐

some cake crumbs ☐   a drawing ☐

[1 mark]

(2) **What does Mum do to knees? Tick two.**

draws on them in felt tip pen ☐

rubs greasy ointment into them ☐

fixes plasters across them ☐

laughs at how muddy they are ☐

[2 marks]

(3) **Look at the first lines in verses 1–4. What do you notice?**

_____

[1 mark]

(4) *She scrubs them with a flannel.*

In this sentence, the word *scrubs* means... (Tick one.)

gently brushes ☐

polishes ☐

rubs hard ☐

pats ☐

[1 mark]

About Knees

(5) Which two words are repeated in the second lines in verses 1–3?

_____

[1 mark]

(6) Look at the start of the fourth line in verses 1–4. **Find** and **copy** a word that is repeated.

_____

[1 mark]

(7) Look at the last word of each line in verse 1. Do these words rhyme?

_____

[1 mark]

(8) How does the poet feel about Mum? Tick **one**.

very angry ☐
a little annoyed ☐
very happy ☐
sad and anxious ☐

[1 mark]

(9) How do you think Mum feels about always having to clean up knees? Use evidence from the poem to support your answer.

_____

_____

_____

[2 marks]

10 Why does the poet suggest Mum should wear shorts next summer?

_____

_____

[1 mark]

11 Look at the last verse. What **four** things will the poet have ready to use on Mum's knees?

_____

_____

[1 mark]

12 Which of these statements about the last verse is correct? Tick **two**.

It has lots of similes in it. ☐

It tries to get Mum to see things from the poet's point of view. ☐

It is longer than the others because the poet has lots more to say about knees. ☐

The first line doesn't follow the same pattern as the rest of the first lines in the poem. ☐

[2 marks]

Akimbo and the Lions

Alexander McCall Smith

This is the start of a story about Akimbo, a boy who lives on an African game reserve, and the adventures he has.

There is a place in Africa where the hills give way to great plains of grass. Zebra graze here, and buffalo too, and if you are lucky, you may also see lions. And at the water holes in the morning, there are other animals to be seen. There are giraffe, awkwardly bending their long necks to the surface of the water; wart hogs, with their families, scurrying in to quench their thirst while nobody is looking; and many animals besides. Akimbo, who lived on the edge of this great game park, knew all the animals well, and their ways.

But now Akimbo was bored. His friends had gone away and it seemed that nothing at all was happening in the game park. His father was too busy to help. He had just been made head ranger and his day was so full of all sorts of pressing tasks there was not much time left over for his son. Or so it seemed to Akimbo.

Akimbo thought about building a tree house. There were plenty of suitable shady trees to choose from, but when he started to look for wood, he found that all the planks which were the right size were earmarked for something else. So he had to abandon the tree house idea.

Then, quite unexpectedly, his father announced over breakfast one morning that he was going to have to be away from home for a few days.

'I'm going over to one of the farms in the south,' he said. 'There have been reports of lion attacks on cattle. They want us to come and deal with the problem.'

Akimbo listened carefully. Lion attacks! He stared down at the table, wondering whether his father would let him go with him. Sometimes he was allowed to go with the men when they went off into the bush on a routine trip, but he had never been permitted to help with anything quite like this.

He watched his father, waiting for him to give more details, but the ranger just sipped at his mug of tea and said nothing more. Akimbo decided that he should ask him straight away.

'May I come with you?' he said hesitantly. 'I won't get in the way, I promise you.'

Akimbo's father frowned and shook his head.

'I'm sorry, Akimbo,' he said. 'I'm going to have my hands full and I just won't have time to look after you.'

'But I can look after myself now,' Akimbo protested. 'I won't be any trouble – I promise.'

Akimbo's father looked at his son. He enjoyed having him around when he had small jobs to perform, but an expedition to deal with marauding lions? That was different. And yet, he had to admit that his son was bigger now, and he certainly knew how to keep out of trouble in the bush.

'Well…' he began doubtfully. 'You won't get in the way, will you?'

Akimbo leapt to his feet in delight.

'Of course I won't,' he said. 'And I'm sure I'll be able to help.'

Akimbo and the Lions

(1) **Where is the story set? Tick one.**

Asia ☐   Europe ☐   Africa ☐   The Arctic ☐

[1 mark]

(2) **Which animals can you find on the plains? Tick two.**

monkeys ☐   buffalo ☐   zebra ☐   crocodiles ☐

[1 mark]

(3) **Which animals are at the water holes in the morning? Tick two.**

wart hogs ☐   jackals ☐   rhino ☐   giraffe ☐

[1 mark]

(4) **On page 85, why is Akimbo bored?**

_____

[1 mark]

(5) **Why does Akimbo have to abandon the tree house idea?**

_____

[1 mark]

(6) **Number the sentences below from 1 to 4 to show the order they happen in the story. The first one has been done for you.**

Akimbo's father agrees to take him on the expedition. ___

Akimbo thinks about building a tree house, but can't find suitable wood. _1_

Akimbo's father says that he must go away to deal with the lion attacks. ___

Akimbo tries to persuade his father to take him on the expedition. ___

[2 marks]

(7) a) How does Akimbo ask his father if he can go away with him?
Tick **one**.

confidently ☐   hesitantly ☐   slowly ☐   quietly ☐

[1 mark]

b) What reasons does Akimbo give for why he should be allowed to go
on the expedition? Find **two**.

_____

_____

[2 marks]

(8) Which phrase is used to describe Akimbo's father? Tick **one**.

the captain ☐   the runner ☐
head ranger ☐   the fighter ☐

[1 mark]

(9) *Zebra graze here…*

In this sentence, *graze* is closest in meaning to… (Tick **one**.)
walk ☐   eat grass ☐   drink ☐   jump ☐

[1 mark]

(10) How do you think Akimbo feels about going on the expedition with his
father? Use the text to support your answer.

_____

_____

_____

[3 marks]

Reading Assessment 3.1 **The Fish in Room 11**

1a Award **1 mark** for the correct box ticked.

very rainy ☐   windy ✓   hot and sunny ☐   foggy ☐   **[1]**

1b Award **1 mark** for the correct box ticked.

bored and frustrated ☐   sad ☐

excited and expectant ✓   angry ☐   **[1]**

2 Award **1 mark** for *deserted*.   **[1]**

3 Award **1 mark** for the correct box ticked.

Toby finds a message in a bottle. ☐   Toby eats lots of cake. ☐

Toby sunbathes. ☐   Toby sets off to look for the lost washing. ✓   **[1]**

4 Award **1 mark** for all three ordered correctly.

Cook's cap **4**

a tablecloth **2**

a wet tea towel **1**

Cook's apron, a second tea towel and the red stocking **3**   **[1]**

5a Award **1 mark** for the correct box ticked.

busy ☐   loud ☐   empty ✓   full ☐   **[1]**

5b Award **1 mark** for the correct box ticked.

happy ☐   bored and angry ✓

excited ☐   sad and lonely ☐   **[1]**

6 Award **1 mark** for each word (maximum of **2 marks**). Accept *chilly, damp*.   **[2]**

7 Award **1 mark** for noting that Toby heard a noise.   **[1]**

8 Award **3 marks** for a complete answer to the question, using evidence from the text.   **[3]**

9 Award **1 mark** for an answer to the question and **1 mark** for a reason for this based on the text.   **[2]**

Reading Assessment 3.2 **Unusual Hobbies**

(1) Award 1 mark for each correct answer.

sweets ☐   shells ☑   coins ☑   sticks ☐   **[2]**

(2) Award 1 mark for each correct answer.

envelopes ☐   pen lids ☑   leaves ☐   ketchup packets ☑   **[2]**

(3) Award 1 mark for the correct box ticked.

paint ☐   use again ☑   store ☐   talk to ☐   **[1]**

(4) Award 1 mark for *soap.*   **[1]**

(5) Award 1 mark for two activities. **Accept** *football, tennis, rugby, swimming, cycling, athletics, surfing, bodyboarding* and *skateboarding.*   **[1]**

(6) Award 1 mark for ninety (or 90) times in one day.   **[1]**

(7) Award 1 mark for reference to the sea being dangerous.   **[1]**

(8) Award 1 mark for the correct box ticked.

Other indoor activities ☐   Outdoor activities ☑

Shopping and leisure ☐   Dance and drama ☐   **[1]**

(9a) Award 1 mark for a correct answer. Accept *riding stunt bikes* or *skateboarding.*   **[1]**

(9b) Award 1 mark for reference to safety.   **[1]**

(10) Award 1 mark for reference to engaging the reader.   **[1]**

(11a) Award 1 mark for the correct box ticked.

to argue ☐   to persuade ☐   to inform ☑   to tell a story ☐   **[1]**

(11b) Award 1 mark for 'other children' (thinking about which hobbies they could try).   **[1]**

Reading Assessment 3.3 Dinosaur Pox

(1) **Award 1 mark** for the correct box ticked.

happy ☐   grumpy ✓   popular ☐   calm ☐   **[1]**

(2) **Award 1 mark** for the correct box ticked.

Nobody knows. ✓   She ate too many vegetables. ☐

She looked in the mirror. ☐   She teased her brother. ☐   **[1]**

(3) **Award 1 mark** for reference to freckles and hair.   **[1]**

(4a) **Award 1 mark** for the correct box ticked.

He is impressed. ✓   He is scared. ☐   He is sad. ☐   He is angry. ☐   **[1]**

(4b) **Accept** *his jaw dropped, wow* or *incredible.*   **[1]**

(5) **Award 3 marks** for all three matched correctly.

complained — incredible

chewing — grumbled

extraordinary — nibbling   **[3]**

(complained → grumbled, chewing → nibbling, extraordinary → incredible)

(6) **Award 1 mark** for the correct box ticked.

meat ☐   daisies ✓   insects ☐   cereal ☐   **[1]**

(7a) **Award 1 mark** for the correct box ticked.

He comforts her. ☐   He chases her. ☐

He teases her. ✓   He runs away from her. ☐   **[1]**

(7b) **Award 1 mark** for an example of Mark teasing Jodie in the text.   **[1]**

(8) **Award 1 mark** for the correct box ticked.

She ate too much meat. ☐   She ate too many vegetables. ✓

She read too much. ☐   She was rude to her mum. ☐   **[1]**

(9) **Award 1 mark** for ticking the correct boxes.

	True	False
Mum runs away because she is frightened.		✓
Dad plans to take Jodie to the doctor.	✓	

[1]

(10) **Award 2 marks** for a plausible answer that makes reference to the text.   **[2]**

Reading Assessment 3.4 **How Do Submarines Work?**

(1) Award 1 mark for the correct box ticked.

It is very big. ☐   It can dive underwater. ☑

It is very heavy. ☐   It glows in the dark. ☐ **[1]**

(2) Award 1 mark for the correct box ticked.

vessels ☐   subs ☐   valves ☐   ballast tanks ☑ **[1]**

(3) Award 1 mark for an answer to the question and **1 mark** for a reason for this from in the text, e.g. *Yes, a submarine is useful during wartime because it can stay hidden.* **[2]**

(4) Award 1 mark for the correct box ticked.

It folds up. ☐

It becomes invisible. ☐

Air fills the ballast tanks to makes the submarine lighter. ☐

Water fills the ballast tanks to make the submarine heavier. ☑ **[1]**

(5) Award 1 mark for the correct box ticked.

captain ☐   chief ☐   commanding officer ☑   crew head ☐ **[1]**

(6) Award 1 mark for *years/years at a time.* **[1]**

(7a) Award 1 mark for the correct box ticked.

to argue ☐   to persuade ☐   to explain ☑   to tell a story ☐ **[1]**

(7b) Award 1 mark for giving a plausible reason for this. **[1]**

(8) Award 2 marks for a clear explanation that doesn't copy the text exactly. **[2]**

(9) Award 1 mark for each correct answer.

	Fact	Opinion
Submarines are really exciting!		✓
There is very little space inside a submarine so it can get very hot.	✓	
It would be fantastic to live on a submarine.		✓

[2]

(10) Award 1 mark for each reason given. Reasons should refer back to the information given in the text. **[2]**

Reading Assessment 3.5 **About Knees**

(**1**) **Award 1 mark** for the correct box ticked.

a sticker ☐   a smear of mud ☑

some cake crumbs ☐   a drawing ☐   **[1]**

(**2**) **Award 1 mark** for the correct box ticked.

draws on them in felt tip pen ☐

rubs greasy ointment into them ☑

fixes plasters across them ☑

laughs at how muddy they are ☐   **[2]**

(**3**) **Award 1 mark** for reference to repetition.   **[1]**

(**4**) **Award 1 mark** for the correct box ticked.

gently brushes ☐   rubs hard ☑

polishes ☐   pats ☐   **[1]**

(**5**) **Award 1 mark** for *how they*.   **[1]**

(**6**) **Award 1 mark** for *She*.   **[1]**

(**7**) **Award 1 mark** for noting that the words do not rhyme.   **[1]**

(**8**) **Award 1 mark** for the correct box ticked.

very angry ☐   very happy ☐

a little annoyed ☑   sad and anxious ☐   **[1]**

(**9**) **Award 1 mark** for an answer to the question and **1 mark** for a reason for this, with evidence from the poem.   **[2]**

(**10**) **Award 1 mark** for reference to Mum being able to understand how the poet/child feels. **[1]**

(**11**) **Award 1 mark** for all of *flannel, plasters, ointment* and *nail brush*.   **[1]**

(**12**) **Award 1 mark** for each correct box ticked.

It has lots of similes in it. ☐

It tries to get Mum to see things from the poet's point of view. ☑

It is longer than the others because the poet has lots more to say about knees. ☐

The first line doesn't follow the same pattern as the rest of the first lines in the poem. ☑ **[2]**

Reading Assessment 3.6 **Akimbo and the Lions**

(1) **Award 1 mark** for the correct box ticked.

Asia ☐   Europe ☐   Africa ☑   The Arctic ☐   **[1]**

(2) **Award 1 mark** for the correct boxes ticked.

monkeys ☐   buffalo ☑   zebra ☑   crocodiles ☐   **[1]**

(3) **Award 1 mark** for the correct boxes ticked.

wart hogs ☑   jackals ☐   rhino ☐   giraffe ☑   **[1]**

(4) **Award 1 mark** for noting either *his friends had gone away, nothing was happening at the game park* or *his father was too busy.*   **[1]**

(5) **Award 1 mark** for reference to the wood being needed for something else.   **[1]**

(6) **Award 2 marks** for the events being ordered correctly.

Akimbo's father agrees to take him on the expedition. **4**

Akimbo thinks about building a tree house, but can't find suitable wood. **1**

Akimbo's father says that he must go away to deal with the lion attacks. **2**

Akimbo tries to persuade his father to take him on the expedition. **3**   **[2]**

(7a) **Award 1 mark** for the correct box ticked.

confidently ☐   hesitantly ☑   slowly ☐   quietly ☐   **[1]**

(7b) **Award 2 marks** for two of: *Akimbo saying he is old enough to look after himself now; he won't be any trouble/get in the way; he will help.*   **[2]**

(8) **Award 1 mark** for the correct box ticked.

the captain ☐   the runner ☐

head ranger ☑   the fighter ☐   **[1]**

(9) **Award 1 mark** for the correct box ticked.

walk ☐   eat grass ☑   drink ☐   jump ☐   **[1]**

(10) **Award 3 marks** for a full answer that includes evidence from the text.   **[3]**

The Demon Headmaster

Gillian Cross

It is Dinah's first day at a new school. In this part of the story, we find out that something more than first-day nerves is making her uneasy.

It was a big playground, full of groups of strange children. No one so much as glanced at Dinah and she felt very awkward. But she was not a person who showed her feelings. Her pinched mouth did not relax for a moment. She looked round, wondering if there were any games she could join in. She thought there would be football, skipping and Tig. And lots of people shouting and telling the latest crazy jokes from Friday night's Eddy Hair Show.

But it was not like that at all. All the children were standing in small neat circles in different parts of the playground, muttering. Carefully Dinah sidled up to the first circle, trying to catch what the voices were saying. When she heard, she could hardly believe it.

'Nine twenty-ones are a hundred and eighty-nine,

Ten twenty-ones are two hundred and ten,

Eleven twenty-ones are two hundred and thirty-one …'

Extraordinary! She left them to it and moved across to another group, wondering if they were doing something more interesting. But they seemed to be reciting too. Only what they were saying was different.

'William the First 1066 to 1087,

William the Second 1087 to 1100,

Henry the First 1100 to 1135 …'

She stood beside them for some time, but they did not waver or look round at her. They just went on chanting, their faces earnest. Behind her she could hear a third group. There, the children were muttering the names of the capitals of different countries.

'The capital of France is Paris,

The capital of Spain is Madrid.

The capital of the United States is—'

'New York,' said a little girl's voice.

'Lucy!' A bigger girl took her by the shoulder and shook her. 'You know that's not right. Come on, quickly. What is it?'

'I can't—I can't remember,' Lucy said in a scared voice. 'You know I've been away. Tell me. Please, Julie.'

'You know we're not supposed to tell you if you haven't learnt it,' Julie said crossly. 'Now come on. The capital of the United States is—'

Miserably, Lucy chewed at her bottom lip and shook her head from side to side. 'I can't remember.'

The whole circle of children was looking accusingly at her and Dinah was suddenly annoyed with them for being so smug. Stepping forwards, she whispered in Lucy's ear, 'It's Washington DC.'

'The capital of the United States is Washington DC,' Lucy gabbled, with a quick, grateful smile.

From the rest of the circle, cold, disapproving eyes glared at Dinah. *Never be too clever,* she thought. *I should've known that.* Her face pinched up tight again as she stepped back and heard them start up once more. 'The capital of Russia is Moscow. The capital of Brazil is—'

Woodenly, Dinah walked on round the playground, waiting for the bell to ring or the whistle to go.

But there was no bell. No whistle. Nothing. Instead, quite abruptly, all sounds in the playground stopped and the children turned round to stare at the school.

There on the steps stood a row of six children, three boys and three girls. They were all tall and heavily built and they were marked out from the others by a large white P sewn on to their blazer pockets. Without smiling, the tallest girl took a pace forwards.

'Form—lines!' she yelled into the silence.

'Yes, Rose,' all the children said, in perfect unison.

The Demon Headmaster

1) a) How do the children react to Dinah when she enters the playground? Tick **one**.

They smiled at her. ☐   They did not look at her. ☐

They chatted to her. ☐   They played Tig with her. ☐

[1 mark]

b) How does this make Dinah feel? **Find** and **copy** a word.

_____

[1 mark]

2) How is the playground different to what Dinah expected?

_____

_____

[2 marks]

3) Why does the writer use an exclamation mark, 'Extraordinary!' to describe Dinah's response to the other children in the playground?

_____

[1 mark]

4) Match the words from the story to their synonyms.

earnest		repeating aloud
reciting		frightened
scared		serious

[1 mark]

5) How do the other children react when Lucy does not know the capital city of the USA?

_____

_____

[2 marks]

6 How does Dinah help Lucy? Why does she do this?

_____

_____

[2 marks]

7 *...disapproving eyes glared at Dinah.*

The word _glared_ means... (Tick one.)

stared in an angry way ☐   shouted loudly ☐

screamed ☐   blinked quickly ☐

[1 mark]

8 *...all the children said, in perfect unison.*

The phrase _in perfect unison_ means... (Tick one.)

beautifully ☐   separately ☐

angrily ☐   all together ☐

[1 mark]

9 What do you think Dinah is like? Use the text to support your answer.

_____

_____

[2 marks]

10 Do you think the six children who appear on the school steps will be friendly towards Dinah? Give a reason for your answer.

_____

[1 mark]

Dear Mum

While you were out
A cup went and broke itself on purpose.
A crack appeared in that old blue vase your great granddad
Got from Mr Ming.
Somehow without me even turning on the tap
The sink mysteriously overflowed.
A strange jam-stain, about the size of my hand,
Suddenly appeared on the kitchen wall.
I don't think we'll ever discover exactly how the cat
Managed to turn on the washing machine
(Specially from the inside)
Or how Sis's pet rabbit went and mistook
The waste-disposal unit for a burrow.
I can tell you, I was really scared when, as if by magic,
A series of muddy footprints appeared on your new white carpet.
Also, I know the canary looks grubby,
But it took ages and ages
Getting it out the vacuum-cleaner.
I was being good (honest)
But I think the house is haunted so,
Knowing you're going to have a fit,
I've gone over to Gran's to lie low for a bit.

Brian Patten

Dear Mum

① **What happened to the sink? Tick one.**

It broke. ☐   The rabbit blocked it. ☐

It overflowed. ☐   The cat jumped in it. ☐

[1 mark]

② *…your great granddad got…*

In the phrase *great granddad got*, the poetic technique used is…
(Tick one.)

metaphor ☐   alliteration ☐   simile ☐   symbolism ☐

[1 mark]

③ a) **How big is the jam-stain on the kitchen wall? Find and copy a group of words.**

_____

[1 mark]

b) **Why do you think the jam-stain is that size?**

_____

_____

[1 mark]

Dear Mum

(4) **a)** *I know the canary looks grubby…*

The word *grubby* means… (Tick one.)

unhappy ☐   friendly ☐

dirty ☐   angry ☐

[1 mark]

b) *Or how Sis's pet rabbit went and mistook…*

The word *mistook* means… (Tick one.)

hoped ☐   accidentally confused ☐

hopped ☐   wished for ☐

[1 mark]

(5) **How do you think the narrator's mum will respond to what has happened? Give a reason for your answer.**

_____

_____

[2 marks]

(6) **Is the narrator telling the truth when he says 'I was being good (honest)'? Give a reason for your answer.**

_____

_____

[2 marks]

(7) **Look at the words at the end of the last two lines.**
What do you notice?

_____

[1 mark]

(8) **What happened to the carpet?**

_____

_____

_____

[2 marks]

(9) **a) The writer intended this poem to be... (Tick one.)**

very serious ☐   humorous ☐

angry ☐   journalistic ☐

[1 mark]

b) Give a reason why you think this, using evidence from the text.

_____

_____

[1 mark]

The Beastman of Ballyloch

Michael Morpurgo

An ogre lives on an island in the middle of a lake. The people who live across the lake in Ballyloch are afraid of him and sometimes throw stones at him, so he has grown up alone and not learned how to talk. But the ogre has one talent: he is very skilled at thatching (creating a roof from reeds or straw). In this part of the story, we learn what happens when the ogre meets someone unexpected.

It was a summer's day and there was a fresh run of seatrout in the lake. Dozens of fishing boats had come out from Ballyloch, and the sound of happy children rippled across the water. The ogre sat on the grassy bank of his island and watched them. He thought at first it was the sound of flying swans, their wings singing in the air; but then he saw her, a young woman in a straw hat.

It was she who was singing. She was standing up in her boat and hauling in her line. Her boat was close to the island, closer to the shore than they usually came, much closer than all the other boats. How the ogre's heart soared as he listened. Nothing was ever as sweet as this.

There was a sudden shriek and a splash, and the boat was empty and rocking violently. The straw hat was floating on the water, but of the young woman there was no sign at all. The ogre did not stop even to take off his boots and his jacket. He dived straight into the icy water and swam out towards the boat. He saw her come up once, her hands clutching at the air before she sank again. She came up a second time, gasping for life, and was gone again almost at once. The ogre went down after her, caught her round the waist and brought her to the surface. He swam her back to the island and laid her down in the grass. She lay there, limp and lifeless, not a movement, not a breath. The ogre called and called to her, but she would not wake. He held his head in his hands and wept out loud.

'Why are you crying?' She was speaking! The ogre took his hands away. She was sitting up! 'You're the Beastman, aren't you?' she went on, shrinking from him. She looked around her. 'I'm on the island, aren't I? I shouldn't be here. I shouldn't be talking to you.' For a few moments she stared at him and said nothing. 'It must have been you that saved me. You pulled me out!' The ogre thought of speaking, but dared not. The sound of his croaking voice would only make him more fearsome, more repellent. The girl was suddenly smiling at him. 'You did, didn't you? You saved my life. But why? After all I did to you. When I was a child I used to throw stones at you, do you know that? I used to laugh at you. And now you've saved my life.'

The ogre had to speak, had to tell her none of that mattered, had to tell her how beautifully she sang. He tried, but of course all that came out was a crow's croak . 'All right,' she went on. 'Maybe you can't speak words, but you can speak. And you can hear me, can't you? My father – you know my father. He's the weaver. You thatched our house once when I was little, remember?

'He always told me you were bad. But you're not, are you? He said you were mad too, that you gobble up children for your tea. But you're not like that at all. I know from your eyes you're not. How can I ever thank you? I have nothing to give you. I am not rich. I know, I know. Shall I teach you how to speak words? Shall I? First I shall teach you my name – Miranda. Miranda. You will say it. You will.' The ogre took her small hands in his and wept again, but this time for sheer joy.

The Beastman of Ballyloch

(1) **What is the ogre doing while the people fish and the children play? Tick one.**

playing with some toys ☐   watching them ☐

eating his lunch ☐   singing ☐

[1 mark]

(2) **What does the ogre think the girl's singing sounds like? Tick one.**

swans flying ☐   cats screeching ☐

aeroplanes ☐   raindrops falling ☐

[1 mark]

(3) **The ogre's 'heart soared' as he listened to the girl's singing. What does this tell you about the ogre's feelings? Give a reason for your answer.**

_____

_____

[2 marks]

(4) **Why does the ogre dive into the water?**

_____

[1 mark]

(5) **How is the girl described just after the ogre saves her from the water? Find and copy two words from the text.**

_____

[2 marks]

(6) How does the girl feel when she wakes up and sees the ogre? Use the text to support your answer.

_____

_____

_____

[2 marks]

(7) a) What does the girl think about the ogre at the end of the extract? Use the text to support your answer.

_____

_____

_____

[2 marks]

b) How is this different from what she has been told by her father? Use the text to support your answer.

_____

_____

_____

[2 marks]

(8) How does the ogre feel at the end of the extract? Use the text to support your answer.

_____

_____

_____

[2 marks]

SAVE THE ELEPHANTS OF VIETNAM

Urgent! Help save the elephants of Vietnam!

It's said that 'elephants never forget'. Let's not forget these elephants – the very few gentle giants that live in the jungles of Vietnam, Asia. Their days may be numbered. These wonderful animals are very close to extinction.

Wildlife expert Barney Long, from the World Wildlife Fund (WWF) says: "Vietnam will probably be the first country in Asia to lose its wild elephants." Soon, all of them might be gone.

To survive, they need YOUR help!

Why are the elephants dying?

Elephants used to live all over Asia and Africa but thousands have been killed over the last two hundred years. The main causes:

- People kill elephants to cut off their ivory tusks. The tusks are sold for a lot of money and then carved into valuable ornaments.
- People destroy elephant homelands by chopping down their forests and jungles. Without their natural habitat, elephants starve. The forests are cleared, the timber is sold and the space is used to grow moneymaking crops such as rubber and coffee.

Why save the elephants?

Elephants are the world's largest and most intelligent land mammals. One of the many remarkable things about these gentle giants is how they help other injured or sick elephants. They are sociable creatures like us, communicating with and caring for each other, and many bond for life.

Incredible elephant facts

- Elephants hug by wrapping their trunks together.
- They are left- or right-tusked, just like people are left- or right-handed. The tusk they use the most is usually smaller because it's worn.
- Female elephants act like babysitters, helping to look after a baby while the mother goes off to eat and drink.
- Elephants can swim underwater, using their trunks like snorkels to breathe.
- Their powerful trunks have fingertip edges so they can grasp objects as tiny as a feather.

Survival statistics

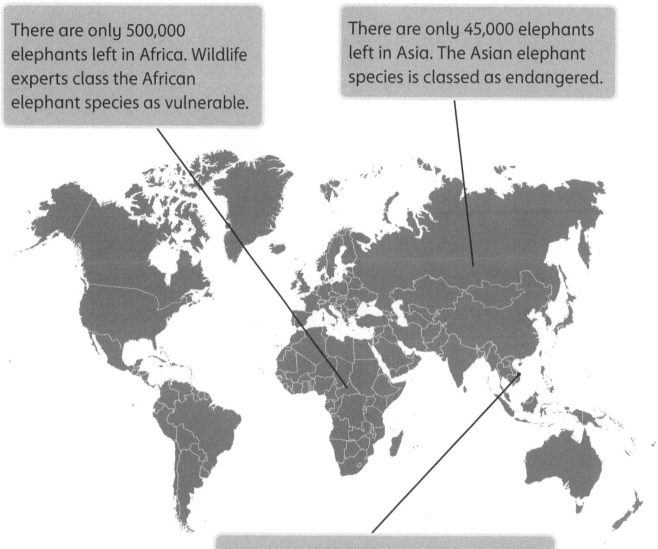

There are only 500,000 elephants left in Africa. Wildlife experts class the African elephant species as vulnerable.

There are only 45,000 elephants left in Asia. The Asian elephant species is classed as endangered.

In Vietnam there are only about 70 wild elephants left (there may even be fewer). They are classed as critically endangered.

Why Vietnam?

It's time to focus on the elephants in Vietnam because things look bleaker for them than for any other elephants in the world.

There are very few Vietnamese elephants left and they have been forgotten for too long. More people know about the dangers to elephants in other countries because they get more attention in newspapers or on television.

Laws have been passed to stop the buying and selling of elephants and their ivory to make money, yet ivory is still being bought and sold. More has to be done.

What can you do?

Don't buy anything made of ivory. People are still hunting down and killing elephants for their ivory tusks in Vietnam, even though it is against the law. These people make lots of money by selling the ivory. Therefore, if people stop buying it, the hunters will stop killing the elephants for their tusks.

Ivory is often carved into detailed shapes, like statues, which are sold as valuable ornaments.

Do more research. Find out more about the dwindling elephant populations around the world. Keep up to date on where and how you can help.

Spread the word. Tell people about the endangered elephants and the few that are left in Vietnam. If you explain that it's urgent, others might help too.

Write to your Member of Parliament. Ask them to encourage all governments of the world to unite against the ivory trade.

Raise money. Do some fundraising and donate the proceeds to charities that protect elephants, especially any that are working in Vietnam, such as the WWF.

Don't let the elephants of Vietnam down. Together we can make a difference and SAVE THE ELEPHANTS of Vietnam!

Save the Elephants of Vietnam

(1) What does wildlife expert Barney Long think will happen in Vietnam?

_____

[1 mark]

(2) Why are the elephants dying out? Tick **two**.

They are being killed for their ivory tusks. ☐
They get ill. ☐
They are not very careful. ☐
Their habitats are being destroyed. ☐

[2 marks]

(3) What is remarkable about elephants? Give **one** thing.

_____

[1 mark]

(4) Why does the writer of the leaflet want us to care about the elephants of Vietnam? Use the text to support your answer.

_____

_____

[2 marks]

(5) How is the situation different for elephants in Vietnam than for elephants in other parts of the world? Find **two** things.

_____

_____

[2 marks]

6 *...class the African elephant species as vulnerable...*

The word *vulnerable* means... (Tick **one**.)

strong and powerful ☐   brave ☐

at risk of being hurt ☐   dangerous ☐

[1 mark]

7 *...classed as critically endangered...*

The word *critically* means... (Tick **one**.)

maybe ☐   possibly ☐   seriously ☐   almost ☐

[1 mark]

8 What does the writer ask the reader to do to help protect the elephants? Give **two** things.

_____

_____

[2 marks]

9 Match the words from the text to their synonyms.

endangered	incredible
donate	give
remarkable	at risk

[1 mark]

10 Who does the writer suggest you write to? Why?

_____

_____

[2 marks]

Cloud Tea Monkeys

Mal Peet and Elspeth Graham

Tashi and her mother live in a village at the base of the Himalayan mountains. They usually go to work at a tea plantation, but in this part of the story, their routine changes.

The next morning, there was no crackle from the fire, no whisper from the kettle, no perfume of sweet tea.

"Tashi! Come here, child."

Tashi crossed the dim room to her mother's bed. Her cough was hard and sharp like a stick breaking. Her mother's face was cold but also wet with sweat.

"I am sick, child. I do not think I can work today."

Tashi ran to the dawn-lit road when she heard the women coming. Two came into the house: her Aunt Sonam, and one other. They felt her mother's forehead and spoke to each other in low voices. Sonam brought water and told Tashi to make sure her mother drank. Then they hurried away to their work.

The next morning was the same. Tashi knew that if her mother could not work, there would be no money. With no money to pay the doctor, her mother would not get well. If her mother did not get well, she could not work and there would be no money. The problem went round and round. It was like a snake with its tail in its mouth and Tashi was frightened by it.

When her mother had fallen asleep again, Tashi dragged the heavy tea basket to the door. She found that if she leaned her body forward she could lift the bottom of the basket off the ground. Bent like this she began the long walk to the plantation.

When she got there, Tashi could see no one; the bushes loomed above her. She could hear the shouts of the Overseer and the calls of the women. She hauled the basket along the rows until she saw Aunt Sonam plucking the buds and dropping the leaves over her shoulder into her basket, again and again, like a clockwork machine.

Before Tashi could reach Sonam, a shadow fell upon her. She looked up. The Overseer stood there, his hands on his hips. Desperately Tashi began to pick leaves, any leaves that she could reach.

The Overseer laughed an ugly laugh full of brown teeth. He called the other women to come and look at this stupid child who thought she could pick tea from bushes that were taller than she was. And then he kicked the basket over, spilling the sad and dusty leaves onto the ground. Tashi looked up into the face of her Aunt Sonam, but there was no help there. Sonam did not dare make an enemy of the Overseer, and she pulled an end of her headscarf over her face and turned away.

Tashi dragged the empty basket down to the shade of the tree that grew out of the rocks, and when she got there she sat and wept with her head in her hands. She wept for her mother and for Aunt Sonam and for herself. She cried for a long time.

Then she wiped her wet eyes with the backs of her hands and looked up. The monkeys were sitting in the circle of shade, watching her. They were all watching her – the babies hanging from their mothers, the older ones quiet for once, Rajah himself sitting looking at her with his old head tilted curiously to one side. So she told them everything. She told them everything because there was no one else to tell.

When she had finished, there was stillness and silence for a few moments. Then Rajah walked through the tree shadow towards her, coming closer than he had ever come before. He stood and was suddenly taller than Tashi. He put his long fingers on the rim of the basket and felt along it carefully. Then, without moving his head, he gave a harsh cry: *"Chack! Chack-chack-chack!"*

Instantly several of the adult monkeys leaped across the clearing, grabbed the basket, lifted it and then, with amazing strength and speed, carried it up and over the jumbled rocks towards the slopes of the mountains.

Cloud Tea Monkeys

(1) **What is wrong with Tashi's mother? Tick one.**

She is hungry. ☐   She doesn't have a job. ☐

She is angry. ☐   She is sick. ☐

[1 mark]

(2) **What does the image 'no whisper from the kettle' mean? Tick one.**

Tashi likes talking to the kettle. ☐

Tashi is being quiet. ☐

The kettle is silent because Tashi's mother isn't making tea. ☐

The kettle is grey. ☐   [1 mark]

(3) **What simile is used to describe Tashi's mother's cough? Find and copy a group of words from the text.**

_____

[1 mark]

(4) **Why is it important for Tashi's mother to work? Use the text to support your answer.**

_____

_____

[2 marks]

(5) **Why is Tashi's problem 'like a snake with its tail in its mouth'?**

_____

_____

[1 mark]

(6) **Find** and **copy** a simile that shows how Aunt Sonam picks the leaves.

_____

[1 mark]

(7) Why doesn't Aunt Sonam help Tashi? Use the text to support your answer.

_____

_____

[2 marks]

(8) What do you think Rajah told the other monkeys to do? Use the text to support your answer.

_____

_____

[2 marks]

(9) Why do you think Tashi talks to the monkeys? Use the text to support your answer.

_____

_____

[2 marks]

(10) Based on what you have read, what does the last paragraph suggest might happen next? Use the text to support your prediction.

_____

_____

[2 marks]

Coming to England

Floella Benjamin

Coming to England is Floella Benjamin's tale of how she moved from Trinidad to start a new life in England. In this part of the text, Floella describes her childhood in Trinidad with her mother, Marmie and her sister, Sandra.

The job Marmie seemed to love doing best was shopping at the local market. What a spectacular event that was! The market was a big concrete two-storey building with steps leading up to it. There were concrete slabs where the stallholders displayed their wares. Meat, fruit and vegetables had to be bought fresh every day. The smell was intoxicating: the air was full of the scent of fruit and spices mixed with a tinge of sea and sun. At the busy, bustling market the noise was deafening. The stallholders tried to outshout each other as they attempted to attract the attention of the customers. The customers, in turn, haggled over prices. You could buy anything there: live chickens, breadfruit, sugar cane, cocoa pods, pineapples, rice, sweet potatoes, sweetcorn, guavas, yams, dasheen, limes, grapefruit, mangoes, tomatoes, cassava and enormous watermelons.

Watermelons have a special association for me because of the day I saw some unceremoniously topple out of a truck. It was on one of the many days when Marmie had sent Sandra and me to the market with a shopping list, some dollars and cents and instructions not to overspend but to get the best things. On the way to the market we saw a stray dog run across the road in front of a truck full of juicy watermelons. The driver had to slam on his brakes so hard that the flimsy wooden sides of the truck collapsed, sending the ripe watermelons cascading on to the road and leaving it awash in a sea of red mush. Shoppers scattered as the melons tumbled down the street – they, like us, could not stop themselves from laughing but the driver was furious. The dog disappeared into the crowd but the red colour of the watermelons stained the road for days.

125

It was also a great adventure whenever we had to buy fish. Sandra and I used to hold hands and skip down the lane to the wharf where the fishermen sold their catch. Fish of all sizes were on sale: red snappers, herrings, butterfish, barracudas, crabs, shrimps and lobsters. Once we were privileged to witness a fisherman's dream – the biggest fish imaginable. It was about three times the size of me.

The fisherman, who was the star of the day, had caught a shark and as customers gathered round to touch and admire the stone grey giant of a fish as it hung high, its vicious grinning mouth pointing to the ground, I pushed my way forward to get a closer look. I came eye to eye with the huge monster, and as I stared back at it I was convinced it winked at me.

126

Marmie sometimes took us shopping in the big towns, like San Fernando and Port of Spain, where there were large stores. There were also furniture stores as well as stores selling fabrics, books and shoes. These were very similar to the stores in any big city. I really didn't like going to them because Marmie would always tell us not to touch the glass counters in case we broke them. I much preferred going to Mr Ching's shop, which was like an Aladdin's cave. It was our local corner shop and sold everything from scrubbing brushes and soap to butter and powdered milk, from shoelaces and matches to sweets and candles.

Coming to England

(1) **What sort of things were sold at the market? Tick one option.**

socks, shoes and tights ☐   meat, fruit and vegetables ☐
books, magazines and newspapers ☐
flowers, plants and trees ☐

[1 mark]

(2) *The smell was intoxicating…*

The word *intoxicating* means… (Tick one.)

sweet ☐   very weak ☐   very strong ☐   boring ☐

[1 mark]

(3) **What was the market like? Explain in your own words.**

_____

_____

[2 marks]

(4) **What trouble did the stray dog cause? Use the text to support your answer.**

_____

_____

[2 marks]

(5) **Find and copy two adjectives that are used to describe the shark.**

_____

[2 marks]

(6) Using the text, tick one box in each row to show whether each statement is **true** or **false**.

	True	False
Shopping at the local market was Marmie's favourite job.		
The stallholders at the market were very quiet.		
Customers were allowed to touch the shark.		

[1 mark]

(7) Which was the narrator's favourite shop? Why? Use the text to support your answer.

_____

_____

[2 marks]

(8) **Find** and **copy one** simile used to describe Mr Ching's shop. Explain the image that the simile creates.

_____

_____

[2 marks]

(9) Why did the narrator not like the stores in the big towns? Use the text to support your answer.

_____

_____

_____

[2 marks]

Reading Assessment 4.1 The Demon Headmaster

1a **Award 1 mark** for the correct box ticked.

They smiled at her. ☐ They did not look at her. ✓

They chatted to her. ☐ They played Tig with her. ☐ **[1]**

1b **Award 1 mark** for *awkward*. **[1]**

2 **Award 2 marks** for children explaining that Dinah expected there to be games, Tig and conversation about TV programmes (the Eddy Hair Show) but instead the children are in huddles reciting things. **[2]**

3 **Award 1 mark** for children realising this shows surprise or shock. **[1]**

4 **Award 1 mark** for all three pairs matched correctly.

earnest   repeating aloud

reciting   frightened

scared   serious **[1]**

5 **Award 2 marks** for children noting that the other children are angry, accusing and smug. **[2]**

6 **Award 1 mark** for children explaining that Dinah gives Lucy the answer to help her.
Award 1 mark for children explaining that she does this because she is annoyed at the other children for being unkind to Lucy. **[2]**

7 **Award 1 mark** for the correct box ticked.

stared in an angry way ✓ shouted loudly ☐

screamed ☐ blinked quickly ☐ **[1]**

8 **Award 1 mark** for the correct box ticked.

beautifully ☐ separately ☐

angrily ☐ all together ✓ **[1]**

9 **Award 2 marks** for a plausible answer which uses evidence from the text. **[2]**

10 **Award 1 mark** for a plausible prediction using evidence from the text. **[1]**

Reading Assessment 4.2 **Dear Mum**

(1) Award **1 mark** for the correct box ticked.

It broke. ☐   The rabbit blocked it. ☐

It overflowed. ☑   The cat jumped in it. ☐   **[1]**

(2) Award **1 mark** for the correct box ticked.

metaphor ☐   alliteration ☑   simile ☐   symbolism ☐   **[1]**

(3a) Award **1 mark** for *the size of my hand* or *about the size of my hand.* **[1]**

(3b) Award **1 mark** for children realising that it is likely the poet made the jam-stain with their own hand.   **[1]**

(4a) Award **1 mark** for the correct answer.

unhappy ☐   friendly ☐

dirty ☑   angry ☐   **[1]**

(4b) Award **1 mark** for the correct answer.

hoped ☐   accidentally confused ☑

hopped ☐   wished for ☐   **[1]**

(5) Award **1 mark** for an answer to the question and **1 mark** for a reason for this.   **[2]**

(6) Award **1 mark** for an answer to the question and **1 mark** for a reason for this.   **[2]**

(7) **Award 1 mark** for noting that the words rhyme.   **[1]**

(8) **Award 1 mark** for noting that the new white carpet got muddy (footprints 'appeared' on it). **Award 1 mark** for giving a plausible explanation of how this happened, e.g. *the poem says this happened by magic, but I think the child in the poem made the muddy footprints.*   **[2]**

(9a) **Award 1 mark** the correct box ticked.

very serious ☐   humorous ☑
angry ☐   journalistic ☐   **[1]**

(9b) **Award 1 mark** for a plausible reason for this, based on the poem.   **[1]**

Reading Assessment 4.3 **The Beastman of Ballyloch**

(1) **Award 1 mark** for the correct box ticked.

playing with some toys ☐   watching them ☑

eating his lunch ☐   singing ☐   **[1]**

(2) **Award 1 mark** for the correct box ticked.

swans flying ☑   cats screeching ☐

aeroplanes ☐   raindrops falling ☐   **[1]**

(3) **Award 1 mark** for an answer that refers to the ogre being happy. **Award 1 mark** for giving a reason such as the word 'soared' implying moving upwards or feeling uplifted.   **[2]**

(4) **Award 1 mark** for an answer that refers to the ogre wanting to rescue the girl as he realises she has fallen in.   **[1]**

(5) **Award 1 mark** for each word. Accept *limp* and *lifeless*.   **[2]**

(6) **Award 1 mark** for an answer to the question and **1 mark** for including evidence from the text.   **[2]**

(7a) **Award 1 mark** for an answer that refers to the ogre not being as bad as she thought. **Award 1 mark** for explaining this by referring to the expression she saw in the ogre's eyes or the fact that he saved her life.   **[2]**

(7b) **Award 2 marks** for an answer that refers to her father telling her the ogre was bad and that he gobbled up children.   **[2]**

(8) **Award 1 mark** for an answer that refers to the ogre being happy and **1 mark** for including evidence of his 'sheer joy' from the text.   **[2]**

Reading Assessment 4.4 Save the Elephants of Vietnam

(1) **Award 1 mark** for an answer explaining that he thinks Vietnam will probably be the first country in Asia to lose its wild elephant.   **[1]**

(2) **Award 1 mark** for each correct answer.

They are being killed for their ivory tusks. ☑

They get ill. ☐

They are not very careful. ☐

Their habitats are being destroyed. ☑ **[2]**

(3) **Award 1 mark** for an answer that refers to one of the following. *Elephants: being intelligent, helping injured or sick elephants, being sociable, hugging with their trunks, being left- or right-tusked, acting like babysitters, swimming underwater, having fingertip edges on their trunks.*   **[1]**

(4) **Award 1 mark** for making reference to the fact that the plight of elephants is more critical in Vietnam than it is in other areas. **Award 1 mark** for including evidence from the text.   **[2]**

(5) **Award 1 mark** for each answer. **Accept** *there are not many Vietnamese elephants left* and *elephants in other countries get more media attention.*   **[2]**

(6) **Award 1 mark** for the correct box ticked.

strong and powerful ☐   brave ☐

at risk of being hurt ☑   dangerous ☐ **[1]**

(7) **Award 1 mark** for the correct box ticked.

maybe ☐   possibly ☐   seriously ☑   almost ☐ **[1]**

(8) **Award 2 marks** for two of the following: *don't buy ivory; do more research; spread the word; write to your Member of Parliament; raise money.*   **[2]**

(9) **Award 1 mark** for all three pairs matched correctly.

endangered — incredible
donate — give
remarkable — at risk **[1]**

(10) **Award 1 mark** for an answer to the question and **1 mark** for a reason for this.   **[2]**

Reading Assessment 4.5 Cloud Tea Monkeys

(1) **Award 1 mark** for the correct box ticked.

She is hungry. ☐   She doesn't have a job. ☐

She is angry. ☐   She is sick. ☑ **[1]**

(2) **Award 1 mark** for the correct box ticked.

Tashi likes talking to the kettle. ☐

Tashi is being quiet. ☐

The kettle is silent because Tashi's mother isn't making tea. ☑

The kettle is grey. ☐ **[1]**

(3) **Accept** *hard and sharp like a stick breaking.* **[1]**

(4) **Award 1 mark** for an answer to the question and **1 mark** for including evidence from the text. **[2]**

(5) **Award 1 mark** for an answer that refers to Tashi's problem going round and round, having no clear beginning or end. **[1]**

(6) **Award 1 mark** for *like a clockwork machine.* **[1]**

(7) **Award 1 mark** for explaining that she doesn't want to get in trouble with the Overseer and **1 mark** for including evidence from the text. **[2]**

(8) **Award 1 mark** for a plausible answer to the question and **1 mark** for including evidence from the text. **[2]**

(9) **Award 1 mark** for a plausible answer to the question and **1 mark** for including evidence from the text. **[2]**

(10) **Award 1 mark** for a sensible prediction and **1 mark** for including evidence from the text to support the prediction. **[2]**

Reading Assessment 4.6 Coming to England

(1) **Award 1 mark** for the correct box ticked.

socks, shoes and tights ☐   flowers, plants and trees ☐

books, magazines and newspapers ☐   meat, fruit and vegetables ☑   **[1]**

(2) **Award 1 mark** for the correct box ticked.

sweet ☐   very weak ☐   very strong ☑   boring ☐   **[1]**

(3) **Award 2 marks** for children giving a reasonable explanation of what the market was like, based on the text. They may notice that it was 'spectacular', big, bustling and noisy and that there was a sense of excitement, commotion and noise.   **[2]**

(4) **Award 1 mark** for an answer to the question and **1 mark** for including evidence from the text.   **[2]**

(5) **Award 1 mark** for each adjective (*grey/giant/vicious*).   **[2]**

(6) **Award 1 mark** for all three correct.   **[1]**

	True	False
Shopping at the local market was Marmie's favourite job.	✓	
The stallholders at the market were very quiet.		✓
Customers were allowed to touch the shark.	✓	

(7) **Award 1 mark** for a reference to Mr Ching's shop and **1 mark** for including evidence from the text.   **[2]**

(8) **Award 1 mark** for *like an Aladdin's cave* and **1 mark** for a description of the image it creates.   **[2]**

(9) **Award 1 mark** for an answer to the question and **1 mark** for including evidence from the text.   **[2]**

Writing Assessment Banks

Introduction

How to use these Writing Assessment Banks

These Writing Assessment Banks include suggestions for tasks that are linked to the *Literacy and Language* units.

Use these tasks flexibly during your assessment week at the end of every half term. Children should have completed the relevant *Literacy and Language* unit before they attempt the Writing Assessment Bank task. For example, children need to complete the whole of *Literacy and Language Year 3 Unit 1* (fiction and non-fiction) before attempting the Year 3 Unit 1 tasks suggested in the Writing Assessment Bank.

All tasks are linked by theme and genre to the writing that children have completed in *Literacy and Language*.

Supporting the children

The purpose of these tasks is to allow you to assess children's independent writing. However, as we want to ensure that children are set up for success, do continue to:

- Set the context for each writing task, engaging children's interest and reminding them of key learning points from their *Literacy and Language* work.
- Talk them through the evaluation criteria to ensure that they understand what they need to do to be successful.
- Allow children to use their notes and plan their writing before they start.
- Help children by giving them ideas if necessary. It is the writing conventions and skills that are important for these tasks, so help children out with the content if needed.

Remind the children that they have been successful once in writing a similar text (in *Literacy and Language*) and that they can use what they learned the first time to write on their own this time round. As with every piece of writing, give the children time *after* they have written to evaluate, edit and proofread their work.

Evaluation criteria

The evaluation criteria for each task are similar to those in the corresponding *Literacy and Language* units. These tasks give children an opportunity to practise key skills in a more independent context.

Use the evaluation criteria as for *Literacy and Language*:

- Look at the suggested criteria and decide which are most relevant to your children. You may want to keep them as they are, change some to particular points that you know your children need to practise, or cut down the number to just focus on one or two points you feel are most important for your children.
- Share the evaluation criteria with the children, so that they are clear on how you will be assessing their writing and what they should pay particular attention to.
- Remind children to check the criteria again when they evaluate their work, and give them an opportunity to amend or add things if they wish.

We recommend that teachers attend the *Read Write Inc. Literacy and Language* training. The training provides further guidance on marking, and how to focus and develop your assessment of writing. See www.ruthmiskin.com for more information.

There are Assessment Progress Trackers online (www.oxfordowl.co.uk) which map the evaluation criteria to the writing objectives in the 2014 National Curriculum. These will be updated as more information about government guidance on assessment and levelling is made available.

Power words

Before each writing task, show children the Power words for the unit from *Literacy and Language*. Check that they understand the meaning of each word. Explain the task they are about to do and ask which Power words they might be able to use in the task.

Timing

We suggest that writing sessions are structured with three key sections – planning, writing, and then evaluating, editing and proofreading. The writing tasks do not need to be strictly timed. (The timing will naturally vary depending on the task and the needs of the children.) For guidance, suggested timings are:

- Planning – around 10 minutes
- Writing – up to 30 minutes
- Evaluating, editing and proofreading – give children the time they require to evaluate against the evaluation criteria, make changes and then edit and proofread.

Unit 1 Fiction

Writing task: A descriptive piece of writing

Ask the children to look at the descriptive piece that they wrote about a beach in *Literacy and Language Year 3 Unit 1*. Tell them they can use this to help them write another descriptive piece of writing about a different scene. Remind them about:

- the words they used to create moods – happy and threatening
- adverbs and adverbials of time
- how speech is set out and punctuated.

Give the children a collection of photographs of different landscapes: forests, jungles, cityscapes, villages, etc. Ask them to choose one of the settings and imagine walking into that place. Will they have a good or a bad experience there? The children should not write a story but a vivid description (either happy or threatening) that will bring the scene alive. It should include dialogue that gives clues to the happy or threatening mood.

Children can use the stages of planning ('build' and 'write' activities) that they found most helpful for their main writing composition in *Literacy and Language*.

Talk children through the evaluation criteria to ensure that they understand them. Remind them that they have been successful once in writing descriptively and that they can use what they learned to write on their own this time.

Writing evaluation criteria to be shared with the children

My descriptive writing:

- includes carefully chosen adjectives to describe and create a happy or threatening mood
- includes sights, smells, tastes, sounds or feelings to create atmosphere.

Grammar:

- uses adverbs and adverbials of time to show when things happen (*At that instant, Suddenly*)
- includes speech which is set out and punctuated correctly.

As with every piece of writing, give the children time after they have written to:

- evaluate their work against the criteria (if they have missed something out, allow them time to add it in)
- edit (make sure that they can magpie from previous work they have done)
- proofread.

Unit 1 Non-fiction

Writing task: An information text

Ask the children to look at the A–Z information text that they wrote in *Literacy and Language Year 3 Unit 1*. Tell them they can use this to help them write another type of information text.

Remind the children of the key features of information texts:

- headings
- subheadings
- captions
- general and specific information
- ordering information.

Tell the children they will be writing a guide to their last class for new children. Ask them to think of all they did last year and what information would have been useful to them when they started. They should make notes as they do this. Children can use the same format as they did to write their holiday A–Z.

Talk children through the evaluation criteria to ensure that they understand them. Remind them that they have been successful once in writing an information text and that they can use what they learned to write on their own this time.

> ### Writing evaluation criteria to be shared with the children
> My information text:
>
> - gives useful information to the reader, for example, *activities to do, what to do if there is a problem*
> - lays out the text clearly to make it easy for the reader to find information, using features such as headings or subheadings
> - includes a picture (or the space for one) with a caption
> - is about the class and is factual
> - is suitable for a Year 2 child to read.
>
> Grammar:
>
> - includes a variety of sentence starters to engage the reader.

As with every piece of writing, give the children time after they have written to:

- evaluate their work against the criteria (if they have missed something out, allow them time to add it in)
- edit (make sure that they can magpie from previous work they have done)
- proofread.

Unit 2 Fiction

Writing task: A playscript

Ask the children to look at the playscript ending that they wrote for *A Tune of Lies* in *Literacy and Language Year 3 Unit 2*. Tell them they can use this to help them write another playscript.

Read *The Night Shimmy** (*Literacy and Language Year 2, Unit 5, CD file 1.1*). Tell the children that you want to put on a play of *The Night Shimmy* but you need a script. Explain that you are struggling with the scene where Marcia comes to ask Eric to play, and after refusing, he helps her with her kite. The children should write the playscript version from this point.

In *The Night Shimmy*, when the two children go to the park, it says: 'They began to talk. Eric found he had many things to say'. Ask the children to discuss what Marcia and Eric might say to each other in the play.

Children can use the stages of planning ('build' and 'write' activities) that they found most helpful for their main writing composition in *Literacy and Language*.

Talk children through the evaluation criteria to ensure that they understand them. Remind them that they have been successful once in writing a playscript and that they can use what they learned to write on their own this time.

> ### Writing evaluation criteria to be shared with the children
> My playscript of *The Night Shimmy*:
>
> - shows what the characters are thinking and feeling through dialogue and stage directions
> - makes links to *The Night Shimmy*
> - is set out as a playscript
> - sounds convincing because the dialogue is based on what I know about the characters in the book.
>
> Grammar:
>
> - includes the suffix *-ing* for stage directions which are verbs, for example, *laughing, whispering*.

As with every piece of writing, give the children time after they have written to:

- evaluate their work against the criteria (if they have missed something out, allow them time to add it in)
- edit (make sure that they can magpie from previous work they have done)
- proofread.

* If you do not have access to a copy of The Night Shimmy, *use another story that the children know well*.

Unit 2 Non-fiction

Writing task: Instructions

Ask the children to look at the set of instructions that they wrote for making a musical instrument in *Literacy and Language Year 3 Unit 2*. Tell them they can use this to help them write another set of instructions.

Remind the children of the features of instructions:

- clear order
- imperative verbs
- subheadings
- adverbs of time and manner
- equipment list.

Tell the children that their task is to write a set of instructions for their favourite playground game.

Demonstrate some poor instructions and discuss why they are hard to follow, for example:

How to skip

First I pick up the skipping rope and put the rope on floor.

Then you can spin the handles and jump over the rope.

Tell the children that their instructions need to be clear. Children can choose their own game but it's advisable to have some alternatives ready, for example, hopscotch, skipping, tag.

Children can use the stages of planning ('build' and 'write' activities) that they found most helpful for their main writing composition in *Literacy and Language*.

Talk children through the evaluation criteria to ensure that they understand them. Remind them that they have been successful once in writing a set of instructions and that they can use what they learned to write on their own this time.

Writing evaluation criteria to be shared with the children

My instructions:

- are clearly laid out, using features such as subheadings, pictures and lists of equipment for clarity
- use precise language so the reader knows exactly what to do.

Grammar:

- includes imperative verbs, to make it clear that I am instructing the reader to do something
- uses adverbs of time (*First, Then, Next*) so the reader knows which order to do things in.

As with every piece of writing, give the children time after they have written to:

- evaluate their work against the criteria (if they have missed something out, allow them time to add it in)
- edit (make sure that they can magpie from previous work they have done)
- proofread.

Unit 3 Fiction

Writing task: A story episode

Ask the children to look at the episode of the story that they wrote about the two robots in *Literacy and Language Year 3 Unit 3*. Tell them they can use this to help them write another episode for a different story.

Read *Cottonwool Colin** (*Literacy and Language Year 2, Unit 1, CD file 1.1*). Look at the end of the story where Colin has got the cat's bell. Discuss with the children how Colin got the bell. Tell them that you want them to write their own episode of the story, in which they are either Colin or the cat, to show how Colin got the bell. Encourage children to plan their episode to include a problem, reactions and a resolution.

Children can use the stages of planning ('build' and 'write' activities) that they found most helpful for their main writing composition in *Literacy and Language*.

Talk children through the evaluation criteria to ensure that they understand them. Remind them that they have been successful once in writing a story episode and that they can use what they learned to write on their own this time.

Writing evaluation criteria to be shared with the children

My new episode for *Cottonwool Colin*:

- has a problem, reactions and a resolution
- has dialogue that sounds convincing because it is based on what I know about the characters
- includes something dramatic, similar to the other events in the story
- shows the characters' reactions to new situations.

Grammar:

- uses a first-person narrator (Colin or the cat)
- includes correct use of the first person (*I, we*).

As with every piece of writing, give the children time after they have written to:

- evaluate their work against the criteria (if they have missed something out, allow them time to add it in)
- edit (make sure that they can magpie from previous work they have done)
- proofread.

* *If you do not have access to a copy of* Cottonwool Colin, *use another story that the children know well.*

Unit 3 Non-fiction

Writing task: A discussion text

Ask the children to look at the discussion text that they wrote about break times at school in *Literacy and Language Year 3 Unit 3*. Tell them they can use this to help them write another discussion text about a different topic.

Remind the children that it is important to consider both sides of the argument to form a balanced discussion. Remind them of any vocabulary they could use to make it clear that they have looked at both sides of the argument, for example: *However ... On the other hand ... Despite this ...*

Look at the ideas that you used in *Year 3, Unit 3, Day 11* of *Literacy and Language*, where you played 'human scales'. Choose one of the following ideas for children to use as the basis for their discussion text:

- Children should have to work for their pocket money.
- Chips should be banned from school lunches.
- Pop stars should not get more pay than firefighters.

Allow children to plan their discussion text. They can use the stages of planning ('build' and 'write' activities) that they found most helpful for their main writing composition in *Literacy and Language*.

Talk children through the evaluation criteria to ensure that they understand them. Remind them that they have been successful once in writing a discussion text and that they can use what they learned to write on their own this time.

Writing evaluation criteria to be shared with the children

My discussion text:

- is balanced (it includes statements that show I have thought about both sides of the argument)
- shares information with the reader in clear sentences that make sense
- shows what is fact and what is opinion.

Grammar:

- includes adverbs and adverbials to show that I am considering both sides of the argument, for example, *However... On the other hand... Despite this...*

As with every piece of writing, give the children time after they have written to:

- evaluate their work against the criteria (if they have missed something out, allow them time to add it in)
- edit (make sure that they can magpie from previous work they have done)
- proofread.

Unit 4 Fiction

Writing task: A poem

Ask the children to look at the poem that they wrote about the water cycle in *Literacy and Language Year 3 Unit 4*. Tell them they can use this to help them write another poem.

Remind the children of some of the key features of poems:

- rhyme
- rhythm
- alliteration
- repetition
- onomatopoeia.

Tell the children they will be writing another poem and that this time it will be about the playground. Remind the children that sometimes the playground might be loud and at other times it might be quiet. Encourage them to use a rich range of vocabulary that will help to show this.

Allow children to plan their poem, considering how they will include different poetic features. They can use the stages of planning ('build' and 'write' activities) that they found most helpful for their main writing composition in *Literacy and Language*.

Talk children through the evaluation criteria to ensure that they understand them. Remind them that they have been successful once in writing a poem and that they can use what they learned to write on their own this time.

Writing evaluation criteria to be shared with the children

My poem:

- uses at least two of the poetic techniques we have studied, for example, *rhyme, rhythm, alliteration, repetition, onomatopoeia*
- uses some unusual combinations of word pairs to build interesting descriptions of the playground
- focuses on the playground at different times of day to show the contrast in sounds.

Grammar:

- uses punctuation and line breaks to show how my poem should be read.

As with every piece of writing, give the children time after they have written to:

- evaluate their work against the criteria (if they have missed something out, allow them time to add it in)
- edit (make sure that they can magpie from previous work they have done)
- proofread.

Unit 4 Non-fiction

Writing task: Explanations

Ask the children to look at the explanation they wrote about why the sea is salty in *Literacy and Language Year 3 Unit* 4. Tell them they can use this to help them write another explanation.

Remind the children of the key features of an explanation text:

- use of the present tense
- clear, detailed information and facts
- pictures
- a glossary.

Tell the children they will be writing an explanation text about how to make an origami chatterbox. Look online for instructions on how to make one of these (or use the short steps below). Demonstrate how to make one to the children, encouraging them to make notes as they watch. Ensure they are given the opportunity to make their own.

1. 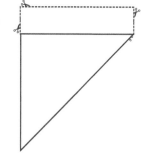 2. 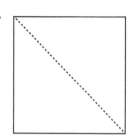 3.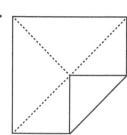

4.   5.   6.

7.   8.   9.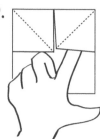

Unit 4 Non-fiction continued

Allow children to plan their explanation using a grid similar to the one below.

Title – a question	
Opening sentence to catch readers' attention	
Main explanation step-by-step	
Closing sentence	

Talk children through the evaluation criteria to ensure that they understand them. Remind them that they have been successful once in writing an explanation and that they can use what they learned to write on their own this time.

Writing evaluation criteria to be shared with the children

My explanation of how to make an origami chatterbox:

- describes a process using clear and useful diagrams, with labels and symbols
- uses continuous prose to explain a process.

Grammar:

- includes adverbs of time (*First, Then, Now*) to help the reader understand the sequence in which things happen
- includes conjunctions (*so, therefore*) to help the reader understand cause and effect.

As with every piece of writing, give the children time after they have written to:

- evaluate their work against the criteria (if they have missed something out, allow them time to add it in)
- edit (make sure that they can magpie from previous work they have done)
- proofread.

Unit 5 Fiction

Writing task: A mystery story

Ask the children to look at the mystery story they wrote about Queen Victoria's baby clothes in *Literacy and Language Year 3 Unit 5*. Tell them they can use this to help them write another mystery story.

Remind the children about the features of a mystery story, including the use of vocabulary such as *culprit*, *suspect*, *clues* and *victim*. Then remind the children about the museum in the *Literacy and Language* story. Explain that this time a valuable painting has been stolen and Sergeant Pemberton, Katie and Adil have been asked to find out who has stolen it. Once again, there are three suspects. Ask children to discuss ideas for what their suspects might look like. Encourage them to avoid stereotypes.

Explain that some clues were left and discuss them with the children:

- muddy footprints
- broken glass from the picture frame (perhaps someone cut their hand while they were stealing it).

Ask children to come up with one clue of their own.

Tell the children that the painting has been found but it's up to them to decide where. As a class, discuss possible locations for where the painting might have been found. Then encourage children to talk through their ideas with their partner.

Allow time for children to plan their story before they start writing. They can use the stages of planning ('build' and 'write' activities) that they found most helpful for their main writing composition in *Literacy and Language*.

Talk children through the evaluation criteria to ensure that they understand them. Remind them that they have been successful once in writing a mystery story and that they can use what they learned to write on their own this time.

Writing evaluation criteria to be shared with the children

My mystery story:

- keeps up the suspense and mystery until the end
- *shows* how a character feels by giving clues, rather than *telling* the reader directly.

Grammar:

- includes speech which is set out and punctuated correctly
- uses carefully chosen adverbs to create accurate images in the reader's mind.

As with every piece of writing, give the children time after they have written to:

- evaluate their work against the criteria (if they have missed something out, allow them time to add it in)
- edit (make sure that they can magpie from previous work they have done)
- proofread.

Unit 5 Non-fiction

Writing task: A non-chronological report

Ask the children to look at the non-chronological report about space that they wrote and presented to the class in *Literacy and Language Year 3 Unit 5*. Tell them they can use this to help them write another non-chronological report.

Remind the children about the features of a non-chronological report:

- clear structure – using headings and subheadings
- extra information using diagrams and pictures with captions
- facts not opinions.

Tell the children they will be writing a non-chronological report about something they are very interested in. This could be their favourite pop star, film star, football player or animal. They should plan the facts they will include and consider the layout before they begin writing. Encourage them to consider:

- which facts they will use in their introduction
- what each section will be about
- what pictures or diagrams they might include.

Children can use the stages of planning ('build' and 'write' activities) that they found most helpful for their main writing composition in *Literacy and Language*.

Talk children through the evaluation criteria to ensure that they understand them. Remind them that they have been successful once in writing a non-chronological report and that they can use what they learned to write on their own this time.

Writing evaluation criteria to be shared with the children

My non-chronological report:

- includes some facts from my notes that the reader will find interesting
- is structured clearly to help the reader find information, for example, using headings and subheadings
- includes extra information in the form of diagrams and pictures with captions.

Grammar:

- includes conjunctions (*and, so, but*) to make the structure of my sentences varied, clear and interesting.

As with every piece of writing, give the children time after they have written to:

- evaluate their work against the criteria (if they have missed something out, allow them time to add it in)
- edit (make sure that they can magpie from previous work they have done)
- proofread.

Unit 6 Fiction

Writing task: A folktale

Ask the children to look at the folktale that they wrote about the wicked enchantress in *Literacy and Language Year 3 Unit 6*. Tell them they can use this to help them write another folktale.

Remind the children of the structure of folktales and the archetypes that make up the plot and characters. Use *Literacy and Language Year 3, Unit 6, CD file 1.2 Think and link* to support the children. Then ask them to complete the planning sheet below or another similar planning sheet.

Features	My ideas
Hero/heroine	
Baddie/villain	
Helper or wise woman/man	
Magic/magical objects	
Problem/difficult task or quest	
Warning	
Special language	
Number 3 or 7	
Talking animals	
Disguise, tricks or trickster	
Lesson or moral	

Allow the children time to plan the build-up, problem and resolution.

Talk children through the evaluation criteria to ensure that they understand them. Remind them that they have been successful once in writing a folktale and that they can use what they learned to write on their own this time.

Writing evaluation criteria to be shared with the children

My folktale:

- includes a vivid description of the setting
- includes dialogue and action that moves the story on.

Grammar:

- includes adverbs and adverbials to explain when and where things happened, for example, *The next evening… On the far side…*

As with every piece of writing, give the children time after they have written to:

- evaluate their work against the criteria (if they have missed something out, allow them time to add it in)
- edit (make sure that they can magpie from previous work they have done)
- proofread.

Unit 6 Non-fiction

Writing task: A biography

Ask the children to look at the biography they wrote of Jamila Gavin in *Literacy and Language Year 3 Unit 6*. Tell them they can use this to help them write another biography.

Tell the children that this time they will be writing the biography of their partner. As a class, discuss the questions that you need to ask to write a successful biography. Use *Literacy and Language Year 3, Unit 6, 14.2 Write 1, CD file 14.3 TOLs* and *CD file 14.3 Write 2* to support you. Once you have collated a good range of questions, ask the children to take turns interviewing each other and making notes.

Children can use the stages of planning ('build' and 'write' activities) that they found most helpful for their main writing composition in *Literacy and Language*.

Talk children through the evaluation criteria to ensure that they understand them. Remind them that they have been successful once in writing a biography and that they can use what they learned to write on their own this time.

Writing evaluation criteria to be shared with the children

My biography:

- includes interesting information, developed from my notes
- includes clearly organised information, for example, using headings and subheadings.

Grammar:

- uses paragraphs to help the reader follow the text.

As with every piece of writing, give the children time after they have written to:

- evaluate their work against the criteria (if they have missed something out, allow them time to add it in)
- edit (make sure that they can magpie from previous work they have done)
- proofread.

Year 4 Writing Assessment Bank

Writing task: A descriptive setting

Ask the children to look at the piece of descriptive writing they completed about the fairground in *Lost or Stolen?* in *Literacy and Language Year 4 Unit 1*. Tell them they can use this to help them write another piece of descriptive writing about a different scene.

Remind the children of the features of descriptive writing:

- the use of adjectives to create interesting descriptions
- the use of similes and the senses to create vivid images
- the use of direct speech, which adds to the scene.

Tell the children that they will be writing about a market/street scene. If children haven't been to a market or experienced a busy street before, you may need to show them photos or video footage. Remind the children to use their senses, memory and imagination.

Allow the children to make notes and plan their writing before they begin. They can use the stages of planning ('build' and 'write' activities) that they found most helpful for their main writing composition in *Literacy and Language*.

Talk children through the evaluation criteria to ensure that they understand them. Remind them that they have been successful once in writing descriptively and that they can use what they learned to write on their own this time.

Writing evaluation criteria to be shared with the children

My descriptive setting:

- uses the senses to create clear descriptions
- uses similes to help the reader build a strong picture in their mind.

Grammar:

- includes direct speech, which is set out and punctuated correctly.

As with every piece of writing, give the children time after they have written to:

- evaluate their work against the criteria (if they have missed something out, allow them time to add it in)
- edit (make sure that they can magpie from previous work they have done)
- proofread.

Unit 1 Non-fiction

Writing task: A leaflet

Ask the children to look at the leaflet that they wrote about keeping phones safe in *Literacy and Language Year 4 Unit 1*. Tell them they can use this to help them write another information text.

Remind the children of:

- the useful advice
- the clear layout, using headings, subheadings, bullet points, etc.
- the use of imperative verbs.

Tell the children that they will be writing another leaflet and that this time it will be about the importance of road safety. Explain that they will need to include information on areas such as how to cross the road safely and how to behave near busy roads. Involve children in a discussion about road safety and, if possible, allow them to watch an appropriate road safety video.

Allow the children to make notes and plan their writing before they begin. They can use the stages of planning ('build' and 'write' activities) that they found most helpful for their main writing composition in *Literacy and Language*.

Talk children through the evaluation criteria to ensure that they understand them. Remind them that they have been successful once in writing a leaflet and that they can use what they learned to write on their own this time.

Writing evaluation criteria to be shared with the children

My leaflet:

- gives clear, useful advice about how to keep safe when crossing the road
- uses organisational features, for example, headings, bullet points, text boxes.

Grammar:

- includes imperative verbs.

As with every piece of writing, give the children time after they have written to:

- evaluate their work against the criteria (if they have missed something out, allow them time to add it in)
- edit (make sure that they can magpie from previous work they have done)
- proofread.

Unit 2 Fiction

Writing task: A poem

Ask the children to look at the poem that they wrote about one particular moment in *Literacy and Language Year 4 Unit 2*. Tell them they can use this to help them write another poem.

Remind the children of:

- the interesting vocabulary
- the sounds
- the pattern on the page
- the images
- the poetic features, for example, *alliteration*, *simile* and *personification*.

Tell the children that they will be writing another poem and that this time it will be about a memory of them doing something for the very first time, for example, starting school, riding a bike, getting a 'pen licence', winning a race, scoring a goal. Tell them that it should be something that involved a challenge. The challenge might have gone wrong or it might have been a success. Engage children in a discussion about any memories they might choose and ask them to share how they remember feeling at the time.

Allow the children to make notes and plan their writing before they begin. They can use the stages of planning ('build' and 'write' activities) that they found most helpful for their main writing composition in *Literacy and Language*.

Talk children through the evaluation criteria to ensure that they understand them. Remind them that they have been successful once in writing a poem and that they can use what they learned to write on their own this time.

Writing evaluation criteria to be shared with the children

My poem:

- describes one particular moment in detail
- creates strong feelings and makes vivid images in the reader's mind
- uses poetic features, for example, *alliteration*, *simile* and *personification*
- is written in free verse, with line breaks instead of commas to show the reader where to pause when reading aloud.

As with every piece of writing, give the children time after they have written to:

- evaluate their work against the criteria (if they have missed something out, allow them time to add it in)
- edit (make sure that they can magpie from previous work they have done)
- proofread.

Unit 2 Non-fiction

Writing task: A newspaper article

Ask the children to look at the newspaper article that they wrote about the lion that escaped in *Literacy and Language Year 4 Unit 2*. Tell them they can use this to help them write another newspaper article.

Remind the children of:

- the chronological order
- the five Ws
- the use of quotations to add detail
- the use of the third person.

Tell the children that they will be writing another newspaper article and that this time it will be about something special that has happened at your school. It could be a school performance, a book day, a topic day or it could be about someone visiting the school. Allow children time to discuss their ideas as a class.

Allow the children to make notes and plan their writing before they begin. They can use the stages of planning ('build' and 'write' activities) that they found most helpful for their main writing composition in *Literacy and Language*.

Talk children through the evaluation criteria to ensure that they understand them. Remind them that they have been successful once in writing a newspaper article and that they can use what they learned to write on their own this time.

Writing evaluation criteria to be shared with the children

My newspaper article:

- is laid out in chronological order (the order that things happened)
- shares the most important information with the reader by answering the five Ws
- includes quotations to add detail or give a point of view.

Grammar:

- uses the third person past tense.

As with every piece of writing, give the children time after they have written to:

- evaluate their work against the criteria (if they have missed something out, allow them time to add it in)
- edit (make sure that they can magpie from previous work they have done)
- proofread.

Unit 3 Fiction

Writing task: Adapting a well-known story

Ask the children to look at the story that they wrote about the Troll and Bogey band in *Literacy and Language Year 4 Unit 3*. Tell them they can use this to help them write another story.

Remind the children of:

- the use of the first person, writing in role as one of the characters from the story
- the inclusion of the character's viewpoint
- the use of adjectives and adverbs to give extra information
- the humorous style.

Tell the children that they will be writing another story and that this time it will be from the point of view of somebody from a fairy tale. You can either choose a story or allow the children to choose. The important thing is that they should be very familiar with the story. Tell the children that they need to choose a character that doesn't usually take the lead in the story, for example, it could be *Cinderella* from the stepmother's point of view, *Little Red Riding Hood* from the wolf's point of view, or *Hansel and Gretel* from the witch's point of view. They should focus on one event in the story, rather than trying to tell the whole story. Allow children time to discuss their ideas as a class.

Allow the children to make notes and plan their writing before they begin. They can use the stages of planning ('build' and 'write' activities) that they found most helpful for their main writing composition in *Literacy and Language*.

Talk children through the evaluation criteria to ensure that they understand them. Remind them that they have been successful once in adapting a well-known story and that they can use what they learned to write on their own this time.

Writing evaluation criteria to be shared with the children

My story:

- is written from the point of view of a character who doesn't usually take the lead in the story
- gives extra information by including powerful adverbs and adjectives.

Grammar:

- uses the first person past tense.

As with every piece of writing, give the children time after they have written to:

- evaluate their work against the criteria (if they have missed something out, allow them time to add it in)
- edit (make sure that they can magpie from previous work they have done)
- proofread.

Unit 3 Non-fiction

Writing task: An explanation

Ask the children to look at the explanation text that they wrote about Jack from his interview about life at stage school in *Literacy and Language Year 4 Unit 3*. Tell them they can use this to help them write another explanation text.

Remind the children of:

- the clear information
- the organisation of the text
- the use of quotations and reported speech to add detail (and how they are set out/ punctuated).

Tell the children that they will be writing another explanation text and that this time it will be about your school. Explain that instead of using quotes from another child, this time they will be using quotes from themselves. Model writing quotes in direct and/or reported speech for the children. Tell the children they will need to write about everything your school has to offer. Allow children time to discuss their ideas as a class.

Talk children through the evaluation criteria to ensure that they understand them. Remind them that they have been successful once in writing an explanation and that they can use what they learned to write on their own this time.

Writing evaluation criteria to be shared with the children

My explanation:

- gives clear information about life at my school
- uses titles and subheadings to organise the information
- uses quotations (direct speech) and/or reported speech to explain about life at school.

Grammar:

- includes direct speech and/or reported speech, which is set out and punctuated correctly.

As with every piece of writing, give the children time after they have written to:

- evaluate their work against the criteria (if they have missed something out, allow them time to add it in)
- edit (make sure that they can magpie from previous work they have done)
- proofread.

Unit 4 Fiction

Writing task: A playscript

Ask the children to look at the play that they wrote about Rumpelstiltskin in *Literacy and Language Year 4 Unit 4*. Tell them they can use this to help them write another play.

Remind the children of:

- the playscript conventions
- the use of dialogue/stage directions to help the actors
- the use of *-ing* endings for stage directions
- the flashback scene.

Tell the children that they will be writing another play and that this time it will be about another character from a fairy tale. (Children could use the same story that they used for the writing task in Unit 3, to save them having to think of another.) The important thing is that they should be very familiar with the story. Tell the children that there will be another court room scene, involving a different character, for example, it could be the wicked stepmother on trial, or the Big Bad Wolf, or Goldilocks. Allow children to discuss their ideas as a class.

Talk children through the evaluation criteria to ensure that they understand them. Remind them that they have been successful once in writing a playscript and that they can use what they learned to write on their own this time.

Writing evaluation criteria to be shared with the children
My playscript:

- uses playscript conventions, for example, names before speech, stage directions and scene descriptions
- uses dialogue and stage directions to show how the characters think, move and speak
- includes a final speech from the judge, deciding that the defendant is either guilty or innocent, based on what they have said in court.

Grammar:

- includes *-ing* endings for stage directions which are verbs, for example, *standing*, *strutting*.

As with every piece of writing, give the children time after they have written to:

- evaluate their work against the criteria (if they have missed something out, allow them time to add it in)
- edit (make sure that they can magpie from previous work they have done)
- proofread.

Unit 4 Non-fiction

Writing task: Presentation of evidence

Ask the children to look at the explanation text that they wrote presenting evidence in *Literacy and Language Year 4 Unit 4*. Tell them they can use this to help them write another explanation text, presenting evidence.

Remind them of the features of an evidence-based explanation:

- causal language
- adverbs of time
- impersonal language
- technical language
- formal tone
- clear organisation.

Discuss some ideas for each feature (see *Literacy and Language Year 4, Unit 4, CD file 12.1 Zoom in on explanations*).

Tell the children that they will be writing another explanation text and that this time they will need to present evidence in court for a character from a fairy tale. Explain that the explanation should be formal in tone and present the evidence clearly (either to establish guilt or innocence). Children can either use the same character as they used in the fiction task or choose a different character. Allow children to discuss their ideas as a class.

Talk children through the evaluation criteria to ensure that they understand them. Remind them that they have been successful once in presenting evidence and that they can use what they learned to write on their own this time.

Writing evaluation criteria to be shared with the children

My evidence:

- has a clear introduction and organisation throughout
- balances strengths and flaws carefully to show that it is reliable
- uses technical language
- uses a formal tone
- includes key words and phrases.

As with every piece of writing, give the children time after they have written to:

- evaluate their work against the criteria (if they have missed something out, allow them time to add it in)
- edit (make sure that they can magpie from previous work they have done)
- proofread.

Unit 5 Fiction

Writing task: A historical story

Ask the children to look at the story that they wrote about the runaways in *Literacy and Language Year 4 Unit 5*. Tell them they can use this to help them write another story with a historical setting.

Remind them of the features of a story with a historical setting that helped to bring it alive:

- historical references
- direct and/or reported speech (correctly set out and punctuated)
- standard/non-standard English for dialogue
- showing not telling.

Tell the children that they will be writing another story set in Victorian times and that this time it will be about a chimney sweep. Explain that they should write about a day in the life of a chimney sweep.

Remind the children about the life of a chimney sweep, using pictures if possible. Ask the children to use their imaginations to describe what it might have been like. Remind them of Victorian dialect (*Literacy and Language Year 4, Unit 5, CD file 2.4 Grammar: standard English*) and how it can help to bring a text to life. Ask them to think about some historical references that could help bring their story to life, for example, horse-drawn carriages, the cold and the dirt. Allow time to discuss this as a class.

Talk children through the evaluation criteria to ensure that they understand them. Remind them that they have been successful once in writing a story with a historical setting and that they can use what they learned to write on their own this time.

> ### Writing evaluation criteria to be shared with the children
> My historical story:
>
> - has characters that seem real because I have used their speech and actions to *show*, rather than *tell*, the reader what they are thinking and feeling
> - has historical references to describe the setting
> - includes dialogue that adds realism to the story.
>
> Grammar:
>
> - uses the past tense
> - may include standard and non-standard English for dialogue, depending on which character is speaking.

As with every piece of writing, give the children time after they have written to:

- evaluate their work against the criteria (if they have missed something out, allow them time to add it in)
- edit (make sure that they can magpie from previous work they have done)
- proofread.

Unit 5 Non-fiction

Writing task: A newspaper article

Ask the children to look at the newspaper article that they wrote, based on life in Victorian times in *Literacy and Language Year 4 Unit 5*. Tell them they can use this to help them write another newspaper article.

Remind the children of:

- the chronological order
- the five Ws
- the use of paragraphs
- key features, for example, headline, caption, columns
- the use of attention-grabbing language.

Tell the children that they will be writing another newspaper article and that this time it will be an article for a newspaper set in the future, instead of in the past. They will imagine that they are reporters in the future, travelling back in time to the present day.

What might children from the future (100 years' time) think of a present-day school? Would they be surprised by the methods of transport that children use to get to school? How would they feel about a school sports day, and would they recognise any of the food in the dinner hall? Encourage the children to discuss this as a class.

Allow the children to make notes and plan their writing before they begin. They can use the stages of planning ('build' and 'write' activities) that they found most helpful for their main writing composition in *Literacy and Language*.

Talk children through the evaluation criteria to ensure that they understand them. Remind them that they have been successful once in writing a newspaper article and that they can use what they learned to write on their own this time.

Writing evaluation criteria to be shared with the children

My newspaper article:

- has attention-grabbing language, for example, use of synonyms to avoid repeating words
- is well organised and includes at least one of the key features of newspaper articles, for example, *headline, caption, columns*.

Grammar:

- uses paragraphs to organise information in longer articles
- may include subordinate clauses to give extra information.

As with every piece of writing, give the children time after they have written to:

- evaluate their work against the criteria (if they have missed something out, allow them time to add it in)
- edit (make sure that they can magpie from previous work they have done)
- proofread.

Unit 6 Fiction

Writing task: A story episode

Ask the children to look at the story episode that they wrote about Hamid on the bus in Pakistan in *Literacy and Language Year 4 Unit 6*. Tell them they can use this to help them write another story episode.

Remind the children of:

- the use of simile and metaphor
- the use of *showing* not *telling*
- the use of dialogue to create tension
- the use of the senses to create vivid descriptions.

Tell the children that they will be writing another episode of *Sugarcane Juice* and that this time it will be about Hamid's father, Abba, as he sets off to find his son. Explain that Abba won't be able to take a bus but will instead use his bicycle to follow the bus. The children should begin their stories at the point that Abba sees the bus leaving with Hamid on it. Tell them that Abba should face different dangers to the ones that Hamid faced. Ask them to think about what might happen to Abba. They will need to consider how he is feeling throughout the story.

Allow the children to make notes and plan their writing before they begin. They can use the stages of planning ('build' and 'write' activities) that they found most helpful for their main writing composition in *Literacy and Language*.

Talk children through the evaluation criteria to ensure that they understand them. Remind them that they have been successful once in writing a story episode and that they can use what they learned to write on their own this time.

Writing evaluation criteria to be shared with the children

My story episode:

- uses simile and metaphor to create vivid images of the setting
- uses the characters from *Sugarcane Juice*
- uses powerful verbs to describe the action
- uses dialogue to create atmosphere and tension.

Grammar:

- includes correct use of pronouns to avoid repetition, for example, *he, they*
- uses direct speech, which is set out and punctuated correctly.

As with every piece of writing, give the children time after they have written to:

- evaluate their work against the criteria (if they have missed something out, allow them time to add it in)
- edit (make sure that they can magpie from previous work they have done)
- proofread.

Unit 6 Non-fiction

Writing task: Persuasive writing (a script for an advert)

Ask the children to look at the poster and trailer that they wrote in *Literacy and Language Year 4 Unit 6*. Tell them they can use this to help them complete another piece of persuasive writing.

Remind the children of how to grab the audience's attention by:

- considering the purpose, audience and message
- using emotive language
- using questions to engage.

Tell the children that they will be designing an advert for Hamid's sugarcane business. Tell them that Hamid's business has really taken off and he is making a television advert for his new drink.

Ask the children to think about:

- a name for the product
- who the advert will be aimed at
- how/where the drink will be sold.

Explain to the children that their task is to write the script for the advert.

Allow the children to make notes and plan their writing before they begin. They can use the stages of planning ('build' and 'write' activities) that they found most helpful for their main writing composition in *Literacy and Language*.

Talk children through the evaluation criteria to ensure that they understand them. Remind them that they have been successful once in writing a script for a trailer and that they can use what they learned to write on their own this time.

Writing evaluation criteria to be shared with the children

My script:

- is attention-grabbing
- uses persuasive techniques to encourage the audience to buy the new drink
- combines text with ideas for images and audio to give a clear message
- is laid out correctly using film script conventions.

Grammar:

- includes at least one question to engage the reader, which is punctuated correctly.

As with every piece of writing, give the children time after they have written to:

- evaluate their work against the criteria (if they have missed something out, allow them time to add it in)
- edit (make sure that they can magpie from previous work they have done)
- proofread.

Curriculum Coverage Charts

Curriculum coverage chart for the 2014 National Curriculum in England

These Progress Tests are for practice, consolidation and assessment of grammar, reading and writing *after* the main teaching in *Literacy and Language*. *Literacy and Language* is closely matched to the Programme of Study for the 2014 National Curriculum. You can find curriculum coverage grids for *Literacy and Language* in the Handbooks (*Literacy and Language Handbook 3* p.187 and *Literacy and Language Handbook 4* p.189) and online at www.oxfordowl.co.uk.

England	*Literacy and Language Progress Tests 3 and 4* are suitable for Year 3 and 4 children who are fluent readers (working at the equivalent of National Curriculum Level 2a and above).

Grammar Assessments

- *Literacy and Language Progress Tests 3 and 4* are closely matched to the Year 3 and 4 grammar requirements listed in the 2014 National Curriculum Grammar appendix (see the overview chart on p.7 and online Assessment Progress Trackers).

Reading Assessments

- *Literacy and Language Progress Tests 3 and 4* draw on the question formats from the National Curriculum Test sample papers and cover key skills listed in the Key Stage 2 Test Framework Content Domain (see online Assessment Progress Trackers). The assessments are also linked by theme and subject to the texts and activities in *Literacy and Language*, to ensure that a context is maintained through the assessments.

Writing Assessments

- The independent writing tasks for children are linked to their work in *Literacy and Language* and allow you to assess children's writing in an unsupported context. The evaluation criteria for each task are linked to the *Literacy and Language* evaluation criteria for writing, and to the 2014 National Curriculum.

Assessment Progress Trackers are available online to enable you to collate your children's results and track their progress against the key areas of the curriculum. You can find them on www.oxfordowl.co.uk in the 'Teaching and Assessment' resources for *Read Write Inc*.

Curriculum coverage chart for Scotland, Wales and Northern Ireland

These Progress Tests are for practice, consolidation and assessment of grammar, reading and writing after the main teaching in *Literacy and Language*. You can find curriculum coverage grids for *Literacy and Language* in the Handbooks (*Literacy and Language Handbook 3* p.187 and *Literacy and Language Handbook 4* p.189) and online at www.oxfordowl.co.uk.

Scotland	Primary 4 and Primary 5 *Curriculum for Excellence* Second level These Progress Tests allow you to assess children's knowledge of a wide range of grammar and punctuation concepts and give opportunities for assessing children's reading comprehension and independent writing.
Wales	*Literacy and Language Progress Tests 3 and 4* are suitable for Year 3 and 4 children who are fluent readers. *Literacy and Language* enables children to become accomplished in: • oracy across the curriculum • reading across the curriculum • writing across the curriculum. These progress tests allow you to assess children's knowledge of a wide range of grammar and punctuation concepts and give opportunities for assessing children's reading comprehension and independent writing.
Northern Ireland	Primary 4 and 5/Years 4 and 5 These Progress Tests allow you to assess children's knowledge of a wide range of grammar and punctuation concepts and give opportunities for assessing children's reading comprehension and independent writing.